A MEMOIR

CHRIS W KNIGHT

CANONIZATION OF SCARFACE

A MEMOIR BY THE GRANDSON OF AL CAPONE

NEW ERA
PUBLISHING

"*The brilliant Swiss psychiatrist, Carl Jung, maintained that personal identity is derived of critical determining factors, among which is the vital archetype of family...the relationships and genetic connections that run deeper than our conscious reasoning. Such is the focus of Christopher Knight's compelling new book, Son of Scarface. Denied definitive proof of his own paternal ancestry, yet defined, in large part, by powerful, lifelong innuendos that the infamous Al Capone was his grandfather, Knight navigates the inevitably complex roads that run among the fact, fiction, fantasy and ambiguity that have haunted him all his life. Son of Scarface is destined to make every reader reflect on the inescapable influences of ancestry on our sense of self.*"

—Jane Delson DICK DELSON & ASSOCIATES
Publicists, Los Angeles

I dedicate this memoir to anyone who has lived through a traumatic life experience. My hope is that you will use bravery and courage in living your life without fear.

Some of the events described happened as related, others were expanded and changed. Some of the individuals portrayed are composites of more than one person and many names and identifying characteristics have been changed as well.

COPYRIGHT © 2008 CHRIS W KNIGHT

Library of Congress Control Number: 2007940159

ISBN 978-0-615-15665-1

Printed in the United States of America

NEW ERA PUBLISHING LLC
300 Park Avenue 17th flr
New York, NY 10022
Phone: 212.572.6317
Email: info@newerapublishingusa.com
Website: www.sonofscarface.com

DISTRIBUTED BY SEVEN LOCKS
3100 W. Warner Ave. #8
Santa Ana, CA 92704
Phone: 714-545-2526 or 800-354-5348
Fax: 714-545-1572
Email: sevenlocks@aol.com
Website: sevenlockspublishing.com

COVER AND BOOK DESIGN BY
Kevin McGinnis

COVER PHOTO BY
Margaret Singer

In memory Ms. Labue our guardian angel.

Please act this
be confidential

TABLE OF CONTENTS

ACKNOWLEDGEMENTS

I have written this book with not only the goal of sharing my family's life story with you but mainly because I want to help make a difference in the lives of young adults and children. I will begin to accomplish this goal by donating a percentage of the proceeds of this book to the Boys & Girls Clubs of America.

I chose this organization because I want to support an organization that enables kids to overcome the kinds of obstacles and neglect that my sister and I faced growing up. The Boys & Girls Clubs have provided a safe haven, caring adult mentors, and hope and opportunity to America's children for more than a century.

I would like to thank the following people for their unconditional friendship they have shown to me while writing this memoir; Shawn W, John M, Jennifer L, Jonathan S, Jennifer F, Mona S, Greg B, MPB, Dr L, Dr C, Dr SP, Jules and Kevin, my fellow friends of Bay Village and to my Camp Posse, Thank You!

I would also like to give thanks to the following people who where there for me as a child when my sister and I were in need of a roof over our head, a meal, a place to go during the holiday's; Justin & Family, Sweet Katie and Aunt Tama, Jennifer/Peter and Family, Connie S. and Family, Nonnie, Cassie and Family, Barbara and John of NJ. Without your past support I don't know what my life would be like today. I don't know if I ever said Thank you, but hopefully you will read this memoir and acknowledge my thanks.

To My Dear Sister, I want you to know that I love you and you truly will be the only person that will be able to understand what all this has meant for us. Throughout it all we have had each other to lean on, we both have accepted each other unconditionally and have tried to heal over our life span by sharing all of the experiences in this memoir with one another. I am so grateful to have a wonderful, caring and supportive sister like you. Thank you!

SON OF
SCARFACE
A MEMOIR BY THE GRANDSON OF AL CAPONE

"Nothing splendid has ever been achieved except by those who dared to believe that something inside of them was superior to circumstance"

–Bruce Barton

Dad

PROLOGUE

"Your father was Al Capone's son."

The man on the phone, Thor, sounded just like the mighty god of thunder from Norse mythology. The way he growled, the words drawn long across a backdrop of sandpaper and splintered wood, sent a chill down my spine. And even if I, at 13 years old, might have suspected such a thing, hearing it spoken without any hint of hesitation made me almost wince.

The truth often did.

I still bore the scars of the physical abuse heaped upon me by a mother half the age of my father. The mental scars were hidden from everyone else's eyes but my own. In time, they too would become as apparent. Each time my mother's wrath crashed down on my sister and me, it felt like a riptide was pulling us under, sucking us back from the safety of my mysterious father's embrace, until we simply drowned in the tragedy of a cloistered life.

Thor didn't say much after that. No one ever did when it came to the topic of who my father actually was. And even as I pursued promising leads—people who had known him, people who knew of him—I would often run into a stone wall of silence, proving that the *omerta* code of La Cosa Nostra prevailed, even though Capone died in 1947. It was almost as if the people I spoke with, and those the various private investigators I had hired spoke with, thought Capone had the ability to reach out from the great beyond and strike them dead with an angelic tommy gun.

"Can you tell me anything else about him?" I asked.

"He was a good man. I gotta go."

When the phone disconnected, it signaled one more wall thrown up in my path. I'd been dealing with obstacles all my life. Forced to play alone in the big house in my suburban neighborhood, unable to interact with any of the other kids for fear of what they might ask about our family, I managed to eke out an existence, at best producing an imaginative mind and at worst, mired in the fear of the unknown.

But while Thor might have ended the conversation, he had done nothing to end the desire burning deep within me to find out the truth about who my father was, and if he truly was the son of Alphonse Capone. Teenagers, after all, are nothing if not terribly stubborn. And as I sat there holding the dead phone in my hand, I knew I would not stop until I had the answers I sought.

I'd come across Thor's number after getting my hands on

the small, black address book my father used to carry with him everywhere. I'd stolen it away from the heap of clothes and personal belongings my mother was getting ready to donate to charity. I still recall the excitement I'd felt while cracking the leather bound book, as if I were at last being granted access to my father's world.

There, on the crinkled pages, I'd cast my eyes over scores of numbers and strange names, filled with wonder at who they might all be, and regret over never really knowing the man my father truly was. I'd only known what he had become: my protector. And now, he was gone.

Determined to discover him, I'd tucked the book away in my own belongings. I would steal glimpses at it during the night under the covers. I could still see my father when he would depart for days and weeks on end; I'd never known where he was going. Or who he was seeing.

At 13, only a few months after my father had died in my arms, I set off on what would become a journey of discovery and frustration. I would find answers to some questions but often, only more questions lay in wait.

Along the way, I would attempt to penetrate the veil of secrecy that had surrounded not only my father's life, but my own as well. I had no idea at the time that the adventure I began in my spare time would someday grow to envelop my entire life.

Mom and Dad 1961

THE SEEDS OF COURAGE

The search for who my father was didn't truly begin until just recently, almost 20 years after he died. Until that time, I was busy dealing with issues in my own life, things that would have derailed my quest had I allowed them to fester any longer.

The root of everything I had to overcome lay buried in the woman I called my mother. My father had been older than my mother by almost 20 years. They'd met and had an arranged marriage that had uprooted my mother from her family and life in New York City, and brought her into the relaxed neighborhoods of suburban New Jersey. Looking back now, it's obvious that she'd felt a great deal of resentment at being forced to give up her life and adopt a new lifestyle to which she forever seemed ill suited.

Combined with the inconsistencies of our life, the furtive nature of our entire existence, my mother had reacted to the stress of this life by unleashing herself upon my sister and me from a very young age. We bore horrific scars of her abuse: knife lacerations across the face and arms, bruises and the continuous mental anguish that fell like an anvil on our young shoulders, forcing us to live in the quiet desperation of children with nowhere to turn.

My sister and I were never sure whether we, too, would fall victim to my mother's almost limitless capacity for rage and neglect, the same way our older brother Simon had when he was only nine months old. We were told that my grand-mother had dropped him on his head on the patio, after which he languished for a week in the hospital before succumbing to the trauma. Later on, my mother insisted that crib death had killed him, but our father felt certain that our mother had neglected Simon's care. My father would often scream at my mother, insisting she had killed Simon.

My father became our protector. Maybe he felt guilty that he had not been able to protect his first son from a horrible fate. Maybe he lived with that anguish on a daily basis. I don't know. I do know that when he was home, he would cook for us and take us to church, and by spending time with us, he would—in his own way—attempt to instill in us the necessary qualities for surviving in life. He planted in us the seeds of courage drawn from his own life, perhaps never realizing that my sister and I were already developing our own form of bravery. We just had to survive the tortuous existence we dwelled in when he wasn't around.

I often felt bad for my sister. Being younger, she was

sometimes forced to stay at home while my father took me, the older one, out to various places like the truck yard he parked his rig at. I have no idea what my sister might have endured while alone with my mother during those times. I only know that to this day, they have nothing that could ever be termed a relationship, let alone a normal one.

Perhaps we should have told our father what was happening, but the minds of children are different from adults'. The shouting matches between my mother and father were already almost too terrible to witness, and maybe I felt that by telling him that she beat us, it would make things even worse. It amazes me how I could justify that illogical train of thought in my younger mind. Certainly, looking back, the best thing would have been to tell him what she was doing, and let him sort things out. But we didn't. And life, such as it was, continued.

Not that he was clueless to the situation. He'd already convinced himself—perhaps rightly so—that my mother had killed my older brother. I imagine he knew that things occurred when he was absent. But, his lifestyle demanded his presence elsewhere, and we were left to fend for ourselves.

As a result, we grew up numb to much of what happened to us. The survival instinct of accepting what happened and trying simply to endure, in the hope that tomorrow would be a better day, manifested itself early in our lives. It had to. The choice was either to endure, or give up and die. And as bad as things got, I don't believe either of us ever wanted to die.

When my father was home, it was almost cause to celebrate. We knew we had moments to be ourselves again; we could pretend we were normal children. And we rejoiced in the chance to spend some time with him.

My father loved to cook us hash browns and eggs, which we devoured as if we hadn't been fed in years. It was, after all, not just the physical food we were starved for, but the mental and spiritual sustenance his presence afforded us. Time spent with my father seemed to have the power to make us believe that we were still kids, rather than punching bags upon which our mother unleashed the stress, rage and animosity she felt over what her life had become.

Because I was older, my father often took me down to the truck yard where he parked. He insisted I come along with him, and he never had to say it twice. The truck yard and time with my dad were the most precious things in the world to me. Being with him when he interacted with the people he worked with, knowing everyone by name and how nice they would all be to me, made me smile and helped force back the sadness that had enveloped my young life.

Since my mother never cooked to any great extent, my father often insisted we eat out. We used to go to a place called the Junction Deli down by the truck yard. It wasn't a fancy place, really just a hole in the wall staffed by some friendly folks who turned out great food. While I sat there chomping down on a ham and cheese sandwich—which was my absolute favorite—my father would joke around with one of the waitresses named Linda. She always brought me an ice cream soda for free, too. It was nice seeing my father talk to a woman without screaming, like he had to with my mother. I think I spent some time wishing that Linda was my mom instead.

The few times my father didn't take me down to the truck yard with him, my mother got paranoid and insisted he was fooling around with Linda. She would often drag us down there in the car, hoping to spy my father in her embrace. But, my father was never there. If he did fool around on my mother, we never saw evidence of it.

My father used to enjoy Burger King a lot as well, but for me, the Junction Deli is where I have my fondest memories of the times we spent together.

We always went to church when my father was home. My mother never attended, but my father, being Roman Catholic, insisted we go. I wonder now if he was trying to instill in us the belief that there was a higher power looking over us. He might have wanted to give us hope to cling to, the idea that there was someone else who we could pretend would swoop in to our rescue us in his absence. "I'm not around," my father might have said, "but God is here, and he will always listen to your prayers."

As time went on, we didn't think that listening was enough. What we truly needed was someone to come and take us away from the hurt and the pain.

My Sunday mornings always began the same way: with my father tickling my feet in order to wake me up. Other kids might have grumbled about having to go to church, but for me, it was more time with our father, and I always jumped out of bed as soon as the tickling started.

Tithing played an important role in my father's life. He always donated a great deal of money to the church. My sister and I attended St. Joseph's from kindergarten until the eighth grade, and my dad always enjoyed speaking with the priests and nuns. He also insisted I become an altar boy, telling me it was important to do good deeds in life.

I wasn't crazy about being one, but because he insisted, I did it without complaint—except for one time, when I was supposed to be at the church for a wedding. Instead of going, I stayed home. Eventually, the guilt became too much, and I confessed to my father that I'd lied. He was furious, and we immediately drove to the church so I could participate in the wedding.

So important did my father consider church and so active was he in giving money, when he died, the entire church and school came to his wake. I remember the funeral home—a beautiful mansion, filled with people coming to pay their respects. It was like the president had died. Hordes of people passed by his casket and shook my hand or hugged me, offering their condolences. I was just shy of being old enough to be confirmed at that time and my neighbor, Deacon Heisenbut-tel, offered to sponsor me instead, knowing how much it would have meant to my father to have me confirmed.

My father was never short on warnings about my mother, strangely enough. When he was getting ready to leave again and we sat watching him pack the small bag he carried, feeling the tendrils of despair lap at the fringes of our consciousness, he would tell us to avoid our mother if possible.

"She's crazy," he would say simply. "Stay away from her and go into the other room if she gets out of hand."

Such advice, while sound, never worked. My mother often chased us about the house, and we would have fled even if our father hadn't told us to. But, she would catch us most of the time and inflict whatever it was she wanted to on that given day. The nature of the abuse was so all encompassing, it's difficult to even recall specific incidents, except the constant horrifying nature of it all.

One of my mother's "favorite" things to do was wake us at 2:00 in the morning, drag us downstairs to the green couch, and strip us naked. She would then bend us over and give us extremely painful enemas. We would scream as she pushed the devices in, crying for our father, but he was never around during those times. My sister and I would shut our eyes and pray that it would finish quickly.

Her rage sated for the time being, my mother would stalk away, exhausted in the wake of her volcanic explosions, and collapse on her bed in a deep sleep. My sister and I used tears to try to stem the emotional and physical devastation that had been wrought upon us.

But even as we blinked away the tears and prayed to God and told each other it would only be a few more days until Dad came home again, we were learning how to survive. And perhaps more than anything else, we learned courage simply by watching my father stand up to my mother.

He would come home from his trips and see the looks in our eyes. He would see the healing scars or bruises, and he would know. And then the shouting would begin.

My mother was quite adept in her ability to intimidate other people, but she had no power over my father. He would stand there toe-to-toe with her, trading insults, shouts, profanity and the occasional slap. We would watch, awestruck, by this display of bravery, for we would never dream it possible that someone could stand up to our mother. To us, she was the all-powerful ruler of our world, unseated only by the random appearances of our father. She cast a shadow of fear over our entire existence and the thought of ever yelling at her or otherwise standing up for ourselves seemed as alien a concept as growing another arm.

But we weren't the only ones who felt intimidated by her. My mother routinely used profanity and threats of violence in her dealings with other people. As recently as a few years ago, Fleet Bank sent her a certified letter telling her in no uncertain terms that she was no longer welcome to bank with them. Their reasons? My mother scared the tellers she dealt with. A visit to the bank often escalated out of control, with her calling the staff incompetent fools and spitting out vicious insults about their families and heritages.

Others felt her wrath as well. Storekeepers who worked in my town came to fear the appearance of my mother in their shops. While other neighbors enjoyed leisurely shopping experiences, the owners dealing with my mother did their absolute best to try to mollify her and get her everything she needed as quickly as possible. In their eyes, the sooner my mother was gone, the better. For years afterward, it took me some time to slow down and enjoy shopping, to the extent that I don't feel the need to run out of the store nowadays.

While everyone else on the planet might have feared my mother, my father certainly did not. He would butt heads with her easily. And the ensuing fights—spectacularly explosive displays—blew about our house like ferocious Nor'easters, usually prompting our neighbors to call the police. I'm certain they showed up at our home at least a hundred times in the course of my youth, but whether they even filed reports is unknown.

Child protection laws being what they are nowadays, I often wonder why the cops never took us into state custody. Surely, they could see what was going on. Surely, they could see the haunted looks in our eyes, or the mottled blues and grays of our healing bruises.

Perhaps there was a grander conspiracy at work that kept them from meddling in the affairs of my family. They'd show up long enough to ascertain that there wasn't a corpse lying around, and then they'd leave again, largely unconcerned with the strange goings-on at the Knight household.

Or perhaps they simply didn't care.

We were the children of a man known as William G. Knight Jr., and his abusive wife, Elise. When our father was working, we were relegated to trying to endure the harsh world we lived in—a world that extended into our early education years as well.

My sister and I both attended St. Joseph's Academy, and it was there that we had to try to make sense of our home life and how it affected our studies. As a result of the abuse, I had to see a speech pathologist until I gradually grew out of my learning disability around the fourth grade. My sister didn't fare as well and stayed in special education classes much longer.

Bullies made my life a living hell. I was the weird kid with the strange family and as such, a natural target for their miscreant ways. They called me names and taunted me endlessly, adding untold pressure to an already over-stressed young boy.

I tried to thwart their actions by telling the teachers what they were up to. At first, it seemed to work, but I inevitably did it too much and ended up getting in trouble with the teachers as well. I had sandwiched myself rather efficiently between marauding bands of bullies and the teachers, who reacted to my overzealous attempts at saving myself by calling me a tattletale.

Physical education classes were especially grueling. Unlike today, the classes were staffed by supposed professionals who knew little about building self-esteem, but knew everything about shaming kids into either performing properly or falling by the wayside. As a result, I was picked last for any team sports. I was the proverbial loser who desperately wanted friends but through the trials of my young life, I was relegated to being a loner.

This isn't to say that school was all hell. There were bright spots, although they were few and far between. My first grade teacher, an old hunchbacked nun named Sister Lorraine, who had the most fragile hands I'd ever seen, would always treat me with a kindness I'll never forget. I suspect she knew there was serious abuse going on in my house, and she did her best to make sure my time with her was joyful. It was too little, too late by that point, but I always felt grateful for her attempts to stem the pervasive despair that she probably saw in me.

My mother was called in frequently for parent-teacher conferences. I think St. Joseph's was attempting to help her work through her issues and end the abuse. My mother refuses to say if this was the case, but I find it impossible to imagine that the administrators would not have seen the abuse going on. Certainly, they should have called in family services if they did see it, but being too young, I had no inkling of how such things worked, and wasn't in a position to demand it, anyway.

There was also the fear of the police coming and taking us way from my father, from whom I certainly did not want to be separated. I probably did my share of clamming up when I should have done the opposite. It's something I think about constantly, but since life doesn't come with a rewind button...

St. Joseph's had a mix of nuns and non-nuns teaching classes. Two of my favorites were the Micucci sisters, identical twins who taught the fifth and sixth grades. They were beautiful and elegant ladies with long, brown, curly hair, who always wore the same outfits. They were incredibly nice and supportive, and always did their best to make sure that I learned a lot and had fun doing so.

I especially remember them helping me through the bullying I was enduring by telling me that I had to learn to stick up for myself. It was a hard time in my life, trying to stick up for myself at school—trying to believe I was worth sticking up for—and then going home to a mother who had no qualms about beating such sentiments out of me.

My sixth grade history class with Miss Micucci was perhaps my favorite of my early years. I enjoyed reading about the great figures in history, being particularly drawn to luminaries like Hannibal, George Washington and Napoleon. As a result, I earned straight As in that class. In the rest of my academic work, however, I barely scraped by, again adding more stress to my life.

Around this time, I met Justin, who would become my first real best friend. We had a bizarre relationship. At school, he would join in with the bullies, keeping up the appearance that he hated me as much as the next person. But away from school, since we both lived in the same neighborhood, he was one of my closest friends. We still stay in touch to this day, and he's married now, with twins. Strange as it was, his friendship during that time helped me get through the sudden tragedy of my father's passing.

In the wake of my father's death, my mother changed. No longer was she the looming specter of doom and despair in our house. As easily as throwing off a coat, she shed her abusive nature and gave us free reign. Where once we had been banned from playing outside and interacting with neighbors, now we could come and go as we pleased.

This isn't to say that my mother turned into a loving, doting parent. Just the opposite, she seemed to view my father's passing as a ticket to her own freedom as much as ours. She no longer felt any real responsibility to look after us and immediately started hunting for another husband she could cavort with. She would scan the obituary pages, searching for likely candidates. She found one in a Greek hospital administrator; she pretended to be a sales agent calling and before long, gained a rapport with this man. They started dating and would go off on long trips together.

My sister and I were left to fend for ourselves, mostly. But, we had a guardian angel named Mrs. Labue, who drove a tricked-out Iroc Z like she was racing at the Grand Prix. She was quite the sight, coming down from Brooklyn to look after us. When my mother would go off on her various excursions with her new mate, Mrs. Labue would make sure we had enough to eat.

High school, then, became something entirely different from elementary school. My sister and I were among the most popular kids at school. With no parents around, we had the best parties, which naturally meant that all manner of drugs, booze and sex escapades were permissible. Coming from the bizarre childhood we'd had to endure, this newfound popularity and freedom was both weird and exhilarating. We felt free, able to soar for the first time in our lives.

I suppose we came close to losing our freedom once or twice when the police raided our parties. Kicking in the door because we hadn't heard the doorbell ring over the blasting music, they found evidence of drug abuse, empty whiskey bottles and beer cans littering the floor, and naked bodies entwined like pretzels, with no parents anywhere in sight. And when they realized that my mother had gone to Europe, they called family services.

But Mrs. Labue saved us. She stepped in and agreed to accept custody of us while our mother was gone. Only by agreeing to give us some semblance of structure did she get the police and family services back off.

The good times continued, though. I drove without a license and forged my mother's name on bank withdrawal slips, to get money out of the accounts so we could buy food and eat. We kept partying. We kept enjoying ourselves.

The only time our fun stopped was when my mother fought with her various boyfriends and lovers. None of them seemed able to tolerate her insanity for any length of time and would invariably kick her out. It was then that she would return to our home, and the harrowing specter of her former self would creep back into our lives. The abuse was less physical, but the shouting continued.

Once, in the wake of a rather extreme partying episode,

she returned and threw my sister and me out of the house for almost three months. We crashed in a friend's basement, not really caring that we'd been thrown out. We were probably more relieved than anything else that she hadn't tried to beat us again.

But Mrs. Labue came and found us, and took us back to our house. I often wonder where she got the money to care for us. When my mother would leave, she'd give Mrs. Labue perhaps $50 to buy food for us. It was never enough, but Mrs. Labue never seemed to complain.

Now, I find myself wondering if perhaps she was another "family" friend who'd been sent to look after us, and was receiving her money from somewhere else. It was well known that she had big, hulking sons who worked in an auto yard up in New York. Maybe, if Thor's theory that my father was Al Capone's son was true, Mrs. Labue was yet another cog in a secret machine set up to ensure that we were looked after, even in the wake of my father's passing.

Who was this woman, anyway? Who or what prompted her to drop whatever she was doing in order to care for my sister and me? Why would she put up with my mother's rude and insouciant ways in order to keep two kids—not her own—safe, fed, and clothed? It wasn't like she was a neighbor. She traveled an hour or two to be there when we needed her. She was also never represented to us as a relative, either.

Strange… But at the time, neither my sister nor I considered it odd or bewildering. Children are children. The definition of maturity is the ability to look beyond immediate gratification and at the time, we were immature. We were still in school, we had needs; this woman swooped in from time to time and met those needs. Good.

Mrs. Labue's appearance in our lives, and various other factors, propelled me to discover who my father truly was— someone beyond the old, grandfatherish figure dressed in a hat and overalls, who the bullies in elementary school used to taunt me about.

But I needed to know for certain.

It wasn't easy. I had scant information to work with. When my father died, my mother adamantly refused an autopsy. She went through the house and gathered up as many of his things as she could find. She donated his old clothes— the flannel shirts and overalls he used to wear while driving his truck—to various charities. Then, she set her sights on his old, chestnut brown, mahogany rolltop desk.

I remember it being filled with papers and files, smelling vaguely of must when I opened it. My mother tore through it, stuffing as much as she could into green garbage bags. When she would go for another bag, I would try to steal away as much of his belongings as I could. My mother wanted to erase all hint of my father ever having existed, but I wanted to hold onto him as hard as I could.

Luckily, one of the things I managed to preserve was his old phone book. I studied the scores of numbers. And while my mother had crossed out many of them—mostly numbers belonging to women—there was still enough to work with.

With the phone book, and a few pieces of my father's history, I began my search. I was unsure what I would find; I only knew that I had to try, if not for my own personal salvation, then to honor the memory of who my father really was.

Thor

THE SEARCH BEGINS

I didn't start right away.

Calling Thor when I was only 13 took a lot of courage on my part. I was just a kid calling up some guy I'd never met, who was named after the Nordic god of thunder. If anything, I knew then that my father had managed to instill some degree of bravery in my soul. And even if our mother tried her best to squelch it out by forever refusing to acknowledge whom we might be related to, or by abusing me, or by simply withholding money, the courage remained planted.

Throughout my teen years, the seeds sprouted. My sister and I were no longer confined to the house. My mother's abrupt attitude change enabled us to enjoy freedoms we hadn't previously. As a result, we grew and partied, and actually began to live.

It was when I graduated college and came to Boston that I again started considering my past, and the many questions I had about it. I still had the few souvenirs I'd managed to save during my mother's purge.

And I still had the phone book.

Logic demanded that I start by calling Thor once again. I had a tenuous connection with him; we'd spoken and he knew my name. Perhaps now that I was a grown man he, would have more to tell me—things that he might have not mentioned to a young boy.

As I pressed the numbers, I felt my heart speed up. The memory of dialing those same numbers almost two decades earlier flooded my mind. Would Thor remember me? Would old age have rendered him a shell of the man he once was? I recalled the way his voice had sounded, the gravelly scrapes, and the rolling thunder of his consonants. Would he still sound that way?

I finished dialing.

An automated recording told me the number had been disconnected. I hung up, feeling discouraged. But then, I remembered that Thor had once owned a rooming house in Flushing, New York. My next stop: the Internet.

Using the registry of deeds in New York, I discovered that Thor had died several years before, but that he had a daughter living in Miami, Florida. I used a popular online search engine to look for her contact information and as it turned out, she owned a horse farm and wasn't hard to track down.

For the second time in as many days, I dialed the phone, hoping to find out information about my father. Again, the phone rang in my ear. But this time, someone actually picked up.

Her voice was soft and feminine. I cleared my throat and began.

"Is Jun Hae there?"

There was a pause on the line. "Who's calling?"

I felt like I was calling and asking for a date. My words tumbled out in a burst of nervous energy. "My name is Chris Knight. My father was William Knight. I spoke to Thor once a long time ago about my father. I was hoping to speak with him again."

"How in the world did you get my number?"

I spilled out my amateur sleuthing techniques and Jun Hae laughed nervously. "You're very resourceful. But my God, I've got chills up my spine right now. Let me call you back."

I sat poised by the phone for the next hour, until at last, Jun Hae called back. I could hear her puffing away on a cigarette. I had one of my own lit as well.

"I remember your father, Chris."

I sucked on the fresh cigarette. "You do?"

"Not well, bear in mind. But I do recall him coming over to our home many times. He had long talks over coffee with my father."

"Okay, let me ask you this: what do you remember?"

Jun Hae cleared her throat. "We used to live in Flushing—you know that from your search of the deeds. When my dad owned the rooming house, your father used to drop by every once in a while. Probably like once a month. Sometimes more.

Sometimes less."

"Did he ever talk to you? Ever say anything?"

"Not much. Mostly just to say hi. But I remember that he was handsome. And tall. Very tall."

I'd never thought of my father as being tall—more of average height—but listening to Jun Hae describe him further, I could see it was the same man.

"He was always very well dressed when he came over here."

"What, like a suit?"

"Sometimes. Sometimes less formal than that. But always tastefully dressed. He never looked like a slouch. He was always well put together."

I shook my head. That contrasted so much with my own memories of my father and his clothes. In my past, the only times he'd appeared well dressed were when we went to church. Otherwise, he was normally clad in faded overalls and a flannel shirt, with an old, dark gray Fedora stuck on his head.

"Anything else?" I couldn't help myself. Jun Hae was being kind enough to help me and I was already pressing her for more detailed information. I realized then that my thirst for the truth had never really wavered, only taken a back seat to the rest of my life. Now that I was starting down that road again, it came back even more overpowering than it had been before.

Perhaps my own appreciation of life and the limited time we all had was what cranked up my excitement even more. Whatever the case, Jun Hae didn't seem fazed or even insulted by my interrogation.

"Every time your father left our house," she went on, "my dad would turn to me and ask, 'Do you know who that is? That is the son of Al Capone.'"

I leaned back in my chair. Flashbacks to hearing Thor say it 17 years previously jumped back into my mind, as if it had only happened a few minutes before. Jun Hae was echoing her father, reinforcing what he had told me so many years prior.

I cleared my throat. "What did you think of that? I mean, was your dad crazy?" If someone had mentioned the same thing to me, I might have suspected their mental state.

But Jun Hae only laughed. "Nah, Dad had all his screws. He was a pretty sharp guy. Might seem like he was nuts, and I'm sure some people thought he might be, but he wasn't."

"It must have seemed weird to you though, huh?"

"Maybe at first, but I thought it was cool, too, you know? Almost like your dad was a celebrity. And him being in our house made me feel almost like a celebrity, too."

"What made your dad think my father was Capone's son?"

Jun Hae paused. "My dad was a big fan of Al Capone. You know the way some people obsess about movie stars? Capone was like that to my dad. He even wanted to buy one of Capone's houses one time. They had some sort of secret room in the basement they used to use for rum running and stuff like that. I think it led out to the East River. My dad really grooved on that stuff. He was a nut for it."

I pressed a little further. "And my father fit in how?"

"Well, I also remember my father saying that your father's mother—your grandmother—had lived in his boarding house, and that Al Capone had paid her rent."

What?! I thought. For years, my father had insisted he'd been an orphan since before he could remember; that I had no living grandparents on his side of the family and that he had never really known his own parents.

"I think," Jun Hae continued, "before your father met your mother, he used to stay at my dad's rooming house. I think they got pretty friendly. Even though my father was older, I think he really enjoyed spending time with your dad. My father used to tell me about how in the forties, Al Capone would bring him gifts for giving William a place to stay."

"And that was it?"

"I'm afraid so. I can't really remember any more than that."

I tore into another cigarette. "But what about records? Are there any left over from your father's estate that might have some more information?"

"That all got thrown out when my dad died. I'm sorry."

I sighed. "I'm trying to figure this all out, Jun Hae. I'm trying to find out who my father was. Trying to make sense of this all. Anything you can give me will be a big help."

"I can't help you any more than that, Chris. Sorry."

"How about some pictures? Were there any photographs taken of my father and your dad?"

"No. Sorry."

The phone went dead and I sat staring at it. Jun Hae hadn't given me much of anything. But for some reason I couldn't explain, I felt like she might know something more. And I wanted that something more. Badly.

I'd been screening several professionals to help in my search, and I called in noted genealogist Mary Ann Boyle, who ran World Data. Mary Ann was an expert at tracking down the heirs to multimillion dollar estates—the kind of people who liked to keep their secrecy intact and could afford to lay false paper trails to discourage the idly curious. I felt that bringing Mary Ann on would be a significant advantage to me.

Mary Ann's company was a small, reputable firm with excellent credentials. People I spoke to about her all agreed that she was an excellent asset to bring in to work on my case. At the time, I was working as the accounting supervisor to a national nonprofit company located close to Mary Ann's office in Boston's Copley Square.

The first time I met her, I didn't say much. I simply placed a photo of Sonny Capone, Al's only known son, on her desk and said, "Don't I look like him?"

Mary Ann remarked that there were indeed a great many similarities in appearance between Sonny and myself. As time would go by, there would be many more similarities than appearance alone.

What I appreciated about Mary Ann was her natural skepticism. She didn't go into working for me with a blind, trusting attitude, thinking that whatever I said must be true. She was a true professional, carefully weighing what little evidence we could find with what I supposed or hypothesized. In the beginning, it was mostly me dumping a ton of research on her and saying, "Here's what I've got; let's try to figure this out." Not exactly an easy assignment, but she poured herself into the case.

For her part, Mary Ann tried her best to disprove Thor's allegations. But the longer she stayed with me, the more she discovered she couldn't prove or disprove any of it. This led to more frustration and eventually, several breakthroughs.

Mary Ann's first assignment was to try to wring more information out of Jun Hae. Within a few days, Mary Ann called me back. Jun Hae had relinquished four names she felt might aid my search for information.

I first tried calling a retired New York City Police Department detective by the name of Frank Coletti. Jun Hae had apparently told Mary Ann that Coletti had hated anything to do with the Mafia, since he felt they gave all Italians a bad name. I felt it was worth a shot anyway.

But Coletti was anything but helpful. Our brief conversation consisted of him telling me that he couldn't remember meeting Thor, but then later on, he did.

"Thor said my father was Al Capone's son. Do you believe that he was?"

"Thor was a crazy guy," said Coletti. "A nice guy, but nuts. He was a big fan of Capone, anyway. I think he would have made up anything if he thought it might bring him closer to the most infamous gangster of all time."

I paused. "So, you think he lied?"

"No, Thor never lied. I gotta go."

I've tried several times since that initial call to get Coletti back on the phone, but each attempt has been met with only silence on his part. He refuses to call me back, possibly because he knows I'll press him on the contradictory nature of his statements.

I next called Jun Hae's mother, who lived in Texas. Despite a thick Korean accent, she had no problem remembering my father. She recalled my mother even more vividly.

"The Turkish woman, yes. I remember her."

My mother was Armenian, but it was close enough for me. And I did not want a minor factor like heritage distracting Jun Hae's mother from giving up any decent information I could use to further my search. "That's right," I agreed. "I'm calling because I want to know all about who my father was. I've got a few theories, but nothing that's truly factual. Anything you can remember about him will really be a big help to me, and I'd certainly appreciate it."

Jun Hae's mother paused on the phone. "Is your mother still alive?"

My mother and I weren't on good terms; if our relationship had been in the intensive care unit at a hospital, the recommendation would have been "do not resuscitate," and I don't think either of us would have argued with the directive.

"She's still alive, yes."

"Why don't you ask her, then? She knows everything. I'm sure she'll tell you."

If Thor thought my mother would be cooperative, he obviously knew nothing about her relationship with me or my sister, or about her parenting skills in general.

"I have to go now, Chris."

I was left holding another dead phone. To be honest, I was getting tired of people hanging up on me. No one wanted to talk about my father or who he might have been, and it was

47

quite literally frustrating the hell out of me.

I had two more names to run down. One of them turned out to be a dead end, but the final name was Rose Pulaski. She was married to a man by the name of Theo Weinstein, a business partner of Thor's in the apartment building in NYC. Rose was now divorced from Theo. Jun Hae thought she might have known my father as well.

I got Rose's number from June Hae, and I called her. She was really nice and agreed to give me the number of her daughter, who was living in Glendale, California, which was where Theo lived as well. I called Theo many times, leaving messages on an answering machine. Finally, one lucky day, his daughter answered.

The reception I got was anything but friendly.

Rose's daughter wanted to know, first and foremost, how I'd managed to acquire her phone number. If there was one thing I'd learned since embarking on this search, it was that you could find anything on the Internet. There was nothing out there you couldn't pull up if you had both the time and the money. Personal information once believed to be private was no longer so.

I told Rose's daughter how I'd found her, and what I was hoping to talk about with her father.

"My father has nothing to say to you," she replied.

"I'm just trying to find some information out about my dad. I need to know who he was—who he really was. Your father might know something that could help me out on my search to find the truth."

She only paused for a second. "I have nothing to say to you. I'm hanging up now."

Had she simply put the man on the phone, had he pleasantly mumbled about how he didn't remember my dad, I would have most likely figured this to be just another in a long line of dead ends. But her vociferousness, her out-and-out anger, the fear in her voice as she pushed me away verbally, only made me all the more intrigued. Who acted that way? And why?

Thor with daughter Jun Hae

Al Capone

AL WHO?

"Your father was Al Capone's son."

That's the line that started this whole escapade, this ripping apart of a young boy's illusions about who his family was and in turn, who he in fact was. My 13-year-old reaction?

"Al who?"

Not as funny as it sounds. I first spoke to Thor in the 1980s. Al Capone's heyday was the Roaring '20s. Check that—Al Capone *was* the Roaring '20s.

It was never my dream to become a historian of some evil Mafia chieftain. I was a young boy pining away for his beloved, deceased father. As years went by, though, I became obsessed with a desire for knowledge, for discovering exactly who my father was and who, precisely, this Al Capone character was—

if he was, in fact, my father's father.

Certain names crop up in our public consciousness as almost mythical figures. We try to compare contemporary figures to them, but it is often a pale resemblance. Every vicious dictator is "the new Hitler." Sorry, but there was only one Hitler and every new despot on the block who kills a few thousand people is not him. The same goes for Al Capone.

The most recent "new Al Capone" was the late John Gotti, but again, the comparison was weak at best. Yes, Gotti was a ruthless killer who ran an incredibly lucrative series of illegal businesses. But at best (or worst), he was the unelected mayor of Ozone Park, a poor neighborhood in Queens, New York.

Capone, on the other hand, first *took over*—took over—the suburban city of Cicero, Illinois, population 85,000, and then went on to take over Chicago, America's Second City, population 2.8 million.

No one ever accused Gotti of taking over a city, nor did "the Dapper Don" have the nerve to make such a claim. But Capone, a native New Yorker—born and raised in Brooklyn—was sent by his early mentor, Frankie Yale, to Illinois to go "on the lam" after committing at least two murders and raising the ire of a rival New York gang.

He set up shop in Cicero and eventually commandeered an entire mayoral election, complete with a puppet candidate and thugs at every polling place. When Capone's candidate won in a landslide, the new office holder had the unmitigated gall to try to stand up to his criminal mentor. Capone personally threw the man down the stairs of Cicero City Hall, in full view of anyone who dared to watch.

Capone's gangs were involved in every known form of illegal criminal activity, including prostitution, gambling, murder-for-hire and general thuggery. But, his crowning glory came in the form of the 18th Amendment to the Constitution: prohibition.

To compare the illegal drug trade of today to the United States' prohibition against liquor is simply unfair—another example of comparing every strong-arm dictator to Hitler. Almost everyone drinks. A small percentage of the populace does drugs.

The 18th Amendment was a gift from heaven to Al Capone. Suddenly, a vice most every American desired was illegal. And when something was illegal, the place to get it was from a mobster. In America's second largest city (at the time), Al Capone's business became one-stop shopping for the old demon, alcohol. His income in the 1920s was estimated to be $100 million a year, not adjusted for inflation.

Not that he didn't have his enemies and rivals. The notorious St. Valentine's Day massacre, wherein seven rival gang members were gunned down execution-style (top that, John Gotti), was Al Capone's attempt to dispose of Bugs Moran, who controlled the action on Chicago's North Side. Moran was tardy—the privilege of leadership—and thus escaped a machine gun's fate.

It was this realistic fear of other gangsters—like being the fastest gun in the West, always being a target for upstarts to the crown—that may have figured into Capone's secrecy in certain matters, family among them.

Capone, an allegedly devout Catholic (how devout can a

murderer be?), was married only once, to a beautiful Irish blond by the name of Mae Coughlin. With Mae, he publicly had only one heir, a son named Albert Francis, a.k.a. Sonny.

Only one child, born to an Italian and Irish Catholic couple, was rather unconventional for the period. Capone had six brothers and two sisters. Mae had four sisters and two brothers.

Sonny Capone was reportedly born on December 4, 1918. My father, William Knight, was alleged to have been born on July 7, 1925—seven years later. But, more on that later.

It was a strange tightrope Capone walked. On one hand, he favored celebrity. He had his own publicist. No reporter covering Chicago failed to have had at least one dinner with the man, usually at one of the city's toniest eateries. When Charles A. Lindbergh completed his famous trans-Atlantic flight in 1927, Capone was among the first to push ahead of the throng and shake Lindy's hand when he arrived in Chicago.

When Capone went to a baseball game, which he loved to do, crowds would cheer as he waved to them from his front row seat at either the Cubs' Wrigley Field or the White Sox's Comiskey Park. There's a famous photo of Cubs Hall of Fame catcher Gabby Hartnett sharing a chat with the mob boss before a game. Since this was only a few years after the dreaded Black Sox scandal, with which Capone's name had been tangentially associated with over the years, Hartnett was called before the commissioner of baseball, and a new edict was sent down that continues today: players were no longer allowed to fraternize with fans once they took the field.

Capone even became a philanthropist. He opened soup kitchens for Chicago's poor and provided daily rations of milk at Chicago schools in order to stave off rickets. Ironically, this particular positive endeavor caused Al Capone to leave another impression on our country that lasts to this very day. Some of the milk given out to the children in his program was spoiled. Outraged, the mob kingpin lobbied successfully for the expiration dating we still see on milk cartons today.

Capone was known as Scarface, much to his distain, courtesy of a switchblade attack while still in Brooklyn. In 1930, Frank J. Loesch, chairman of the Chicago Crime Commission, compiled a list of "public enemies" whom he saw as corrupting the city. The list was published worldwide. The name at the top? The first "public enemy number one": Alphonse Gabriel Capone.

His likeness and name have been featured in at least 13 major motion pictures. The television series *The Untouchables* and its spin-off movies revolved around real-life do-gooder Eliot Ness and his battle with the evil Al Capone. Unlike more thinly veiled characters in the book *The Godfather*, Capone is featured by name.

In short, what Babe Ruth was to baseball, what Adolph Hitler was to genocide and dictatorship, what the Beatles were to popular music, Al Capone was to crime.

You mean to tell me I'm *related* to this man?

It's a strange concept to wrap one's mind around. Times have changed. Capone's son, the man who went through life as Sonny Capone, did everything in his power to shy away from his father's spotlight and infamy. He went to college, became a florist, and served his country as an airplane mechanic's apprentice during the war. Eventually, he even changed his name to Albert Francis, his first and middle names. Obviously, the man did everything he could to keep a low profile.

As a society, we get different messages in different eras. In the Broadway musical *Chicago*, the Roaring '20s are depicted as a time when notoriety was every bit as good as fame. Was it? Not for the man known publicly as Sonny Capone.

Today, we have cable reality shows like *Growing Up Gotti*. The Teflon Don's bleached-blond daughter never saw a camera or a reporter she didn't like or try to glom on to. As the saying goes, there is no such thing as bad publicity—just spell the name right. Reality shows in general are the greatest manifestation of Andy Warhol's claim that in the future, we all will be famous for 15 minutes.

All of this was farther than far from my mind, though. I don't want to be famous. Discovering Al Capone's identity and lore were important to my journey, my search for truth and, perhaps, closure. But I've no doubt I would have pursued this venture with the same fervor if I'd been told my real father was the garbage man down the street. I just had to know, deep inside my heart and mind. When doubt, realistic doubt, crops up in your consciousness, you simply have to know.

Al Capones Florida Estate

V

THE MISSING YEARS

While I started discussing options with Mark the private investigator—specifically, the need for a trip to California—Mary Ann, my genealogist, was already working feverishly to trace various papers and records she felt might have importance in the case.

Mary Ann assembled a crack team of professionals and subcontractors to help, all of whom were supremely adept at their jobs. As she would later tell me, it was like casting a giant net out into the universe. Sooner or later, nuggets of information would get caught in it that would help us unravel this thing.

My father had once told me that his parents had died in a plane crash when he was very young. And yet, working backward in time, Mary Ann could find no news anywhere about a plane crash. This struck her as odd, considering that at the time, airline travel would have been fairly new. A crash would have certainly made the papers.

She also theorized that if my father's parents had been killed in a plane crash, they would have been fairly wealthy, since airline travel in the early part of the 20th century would have been prohibitively expensive for just anyone.

But no records existed of any plane crash in the Cook County, Illinois, area. Old microfiche catalogs, mimeographed sheets of old town news, city papers—none of it held any mention of a plane crash.

Expanding her search outward, Mary Ann started tracking the last name of my grandmother, found on my father's birth certificate: Irene Maude Meis. In the Cook County area, where my father supposedly had first popped his head out, there was a very well to do family named Meis, who owned a chain of department stores. Despite searching extensively, Mary Ann was unable to find a connection between my father's mother and this one. She wondered if this was simply the result of someone assuming another family's name to make themselves possibly look better.

Mary Ann went back further in time and attempted to locate a birth certificate on my father's mother, but found nothing. Granted, birth certificates were not required for a newborn at that point in history, so it's a bit of a loophole that might have been exploited by someone who knew how to work the system to their advantage. Mary Ann was only able to conclude that there seemed to be nothing to link anyone named Meis with my father's father, who supposedly was named William Knight also.

My grandfather, William Knight, Sr., was allegedly born in Ohio, according to my father's birth certificate. It also had him listed as a traveling salesman, but otherwise, there's very little documentation on this particular person. Mary Ann and her crack team of seasoned professionals cast a huge net all over the Midwest, attempting to locate other William Knights. Unfortunately, any that she was able to turn up could not be identified as my grandfather.

Up to that point, Mary Ann had relied on trusted associates to discover this information. But, not wanting to discount the possibility of human error, she journeyed to Illinois to run down the leads herself, as any excellent private investigator might be inclined to do. She had no expectations for the trip; she didn't necessarily expect to break the case wide open. Before she went, she was resigned, and reasoned that possibly, there was nothing she could do.

A few months went by and I begged her to stay onboard, to help solve this festering mystery that I could not put to sleep. Everything she turned up led to the same result. She spoke with the city clerk and the county clerk, who both confirmed that because birth certificates weren't required, trying to find the origin of someone would be a very difficult task indeed.

Mary Ann was forced, therefore, to consider several possibilities.

First, did a young woman get herself into trouble, find out she was pregnant and possibly borrow the last name of Meis from some well connected, upstanding members of Cook County society? Or was there a deeper level of impersonation going on? It was possible, Mary Ann concluded, for a transient young woman falling on hard times to take the name, but was it likely? Meis wasn't a common name like Smith or Jones, and it seemed far more likely that a woman might choose something more common if she were embarrassed about her situation.

The second option was that Al Capone, who was reputed to have had several girlfriends at varying times in his criminal career, might have impregnated one of them and, realizing the precarious nature of the situation, used a little bit of his influence to set the woman up with everything she needed, including money, a place to stay and fraudulent papers.

Given Capone's extreme power, particularly in this very same part of the country, fabricating a phony birth certificate would have been an easy task. I think it would simply be a matter of finding a country doctor in need of some extra cash, waving a huge pile of greenbacks in front of him, and presto— fake birth certificate. I often wonder if there were other children scattered to the winds like that, with no real pasts, who simply disappeared into the extensive foster child network that sprouted during those incredibly difficult years of the Great Depression.

How easy would it have been to alter paperwork, forget to file some records, or even write down the wrong name? I think, almost ridiculously so. One could have found many people so desperate for money that someone could have offered a dime for such services and still gotten a nickel in change. When times are tough, money is the biggest motivator of all, and money during the Depression was coveted like no other time in American history.

There are a few flaws to this theory, though—or, shall I

say, a few possible variations, some of which seem more plausible than others.

The implication that Capone impregnated a girlfriend, and then set her and the child up, flew in the face of what little facts I'd uncovered. The closest I came to anyone talking about Capone having a "kept woman with child" was Jun Hae's comment about Scarface paying the rent for "my father's mother" at Thor's boarding house.

What worked against this theory were two things: one logistical, the other, psychological, and both tended to overlap. Logistically, had there been a mother on the scene, a Capone gun moll who was really my paternal grandmother, then why did my father have no recollection of such a woman? Why would he hide her from our lives? It would be one thing to run from the Capone lineage, but a completely other issue to run from whomever was his birth mother. When asked for next-of-kin contacts early on in his life, why did my father never mention a living mother? Why did it appear that he never lived with one?

Also, Capone biographers have mentioned numerous girlfriends and mistresses. None was said to have been with child, or to have had a child with Capone. He had a dichotomous public image: the faithful family man with one male child on one hand; on the other, his longtime girlfriends, his marital unfaithfulness, were perhaps not front page news, but they were far from well kept secrets in certain circles. Yet, those circles never spoke of a bastard child.

The more plausible theory would have been that Capone impregnated a woman, and then sent the baby away *sans* mother. This theory, too, had problems. Capone and his brothers—Ralph, Frank, John, Albert and Matthew, the ones who also resided within Al's world of criminal activity—were infamous for getting floozies "in the family way" and then forcing them to have back-alley abortions, despite the men's alleged devout Catholicism. So, why choose to allow one girlfriend to *have* a baby and then send it away?

If the theory were to continue to fruition, and Capone also "took care" of the child financially and otherwise, would he not have done a better job of it? Wouldn't he have set my father up with a nice family from the get-go, living in placid, suburban splendor, going to the best schools and such? But this was not my father's lot in life—at least, not as he initially told of it.

If one were to buy into the theory that my father was the progeny of Al Capone, the most logical theory at this juncture might have been that one of "his girls" got pregnant and did not inform Public Enemy Number One for fear of a crude abortion, which would put her own life in great peril as well. After giving birth, she may have then sought out some meager assistance from the man in order to arrive at a mutually benefi-cial arrange-ment: Al would "bury" their joint indiscretion by creating a phony birth certificate, slip the mother a few bucks to keep quiet and go about her business, and then check in to bestow upon the young child and/or his foster parents a few dollars, to ensure that the kid not starve to death. A Magwitch to my father's Pip.

This might also have explained one obvious question: how did my father ever come to know or imagine that he was Al Capone's son? For where else but from my own father could such a series of rumors have spread? Unless somehow it had all come back to Thor, who may have reached out to my father as my father grew older, to share the knowledge that Capone's mistress—my father's mother—had been one of his rooming house tenants.

My mind was beginning to reel.

Mary Ann kept running the Meis name down. She had a good friend—a census professional—who traced it back to a French-Jewish family that had settled for a few years in New York. But, they never seemed to go beyond New York. This particular Meis family had no connection to Illinois.

Mary Ann also used the contacts on my father's Social Security application, but to no avail. Already, things that might be commonplace in a modern society were missing from his early years. It was almost as if someone had jotted down some names with no real background whatsoever.

One strange item appeared on that Social Security application, though. On it, my father listed his mother as "unknown." How had this come to pass? Was he not aware of the existence of his own birth certificate? It was possible. My father was 19 when he applied for a Social Security card. It brought to mind the old Watergate phrase: "What did he know and when did he know it?" Perhaps he had no idea of his birth mother's name; perhaps he had for some reason repudiated her, as I had so often wished I'd done to mine.

Mary Ann also tracked down the address where Irene Meis was said to have been living at the time of my father's birth. There was a family there by the name of Altenburg, not Meis. August Altenburg died of natural causes at the age of 70, in 1929. His wife, Betsy, committed suicide at the age of 72, in 1935. These two were certainly too old to have conceived my father in 1925, and might also have been too old to have even been his grandparents. But they may have been the right ages to have been his birth mother's grandparents, and grandparents may have been a safe haven for a pregnant-out-of-wedlock young girl, such as 19-year-old Irene Maude Meis.

Mary Ann needed to find the farm where my father had claimed he'd spent some years in his youth. She drove out along the one-lane, country roads of rural Illinois, her rental car kicking up whorls of dust in her wake as she passed field after field of cornrows. The endless miles of wooden slat fences, the chicken wire and the red-tailed hawks drawing lazy circles in the sky almost lulled her to sleep several times. But, eventually, she found the nearest town to where the farm was supposedly situated.

She stopped by the post office and eventually managed to get friendly with a worker. He couldn't help her, but suggested she head down to the local coffee house-cum-diner, where a lot of the old locals hung out.

Mary Ann found the diner—little more than a hole in the wall, with crinkled, yellow menus and chipped laminate table-tops. The greasy spatula-wielding cook suggested she wait an hour or so, because some of the older locals would be around and they might be able to direct her to the farm. Sure enough, like a rusty old clock, several grizzled old-timers pushed their way through the creaking doors and ordered their usual breakfast of eggs, grits and bacon, along with black-as-night coffee.

The locals had an instant distrust of strangers, the way some folks are liable to be when they spot an out-of-town car nuzzling up to their favorite watering hole. But Mary Ann, being a Midwesterner herself, knew how to speak their language, and developed an instant rapport with the old geezers. They saw that she wasn't just a city slicker out prospecting cheap land for sale, intent on turning their slice of rural utopia into the next suburban nightmare, but a woman on a mission. They agreed to give her directions to the farm. She later told me that if they hadn't helped, she might well be out there still searching for the farm, it was so far off the beaten track.

Mary Ann found her way down a road pockmarked by tree roots, and bits of old-time asphalt broken up by nature trying to reclaim its birthright. Her car jumped and clanged over the bumps in the road, scraping the undercarriage as she drove, until at last she came to a break in the fence line. She turned down a side road that was little more than hard-packed dirt edged with tall grass and chickweed, and followed it as it wound for almost a mile, past acres and acres of farmland.

At last, in front of her, she could make out the farmhouse. White paint flecked off it by the foundation and she could see a spare shutter banging against the house as a vague summer breeze kicked it about. It all seemed quiet, and Mary Ann wondered if anyone still lived there. If she hadn't noticed that the fields looked well cared for, she might have suspected it was long since abandoned.

The farm was once owned by James and Lillian Buzick. According to my father, he'd simply showed up there one warm day in the spring of 1941, although this date appeared questionable; it's highly possible he landed there as early as 1937, when he was only 12 years old. The Buzicks, being gracious people, gladly took him in, and that was it: my father showed up and they took him in. I've never understood how complete strangers could simply do that, and it's one of the many aspects of my father's life that still leaves me buzzing with questions.

My father spent the next few years working on the farm before enlisting in the US Navy. But what irked Mary Ann and annoyed me was the fact that for the years between his birth and when he appeared at the Buzicks, there were no records of him. There were no records, no pictures, no nothing. It was as if my father had existed on paper in 1925, when his official birth certificate recorded his appearance in this world, and then in the flesh somewhere between 1937 and 1941.

Of course, that was if his birth certificate was even legitimate. My father had told me several times that he was actually born in 1917 or 1918—the same year as the man known as Sonny Capone—and had altered his birth certificate later on. I used to ask him why, but he would simply brush my questions off, telling me that he had good reasons for doing so. As I'd come to find out, more and more things about my father's past were done for good reasons, but I could never seem to discover what those reasons were.

Whether he was born in 1917, 1918 or 1925, before 1941, I had no idea where he might have been. At varying times in my own youth, he'd told me that he'd had a tumultuous childhood, being tossed from foster home to foster home, sometimes at the mercy of deranged drunks who would beat him, and he'd go hungry for days on end, wondering if he'd ever see a morsel of food again.

But at other times, he would speak of an amazing childhood spent growing up in a beautiful mansion in Florida, resplendent with handwoven tapestries hanging on the walls, a glistening pond filled with crimson carp lolling in the green water reeds, luxury automobiles that shone in the tropical sunlight, and fresh fruit served everyday at breakfast, on silver platters polished to a mirror-like finish.

That was the kind of place where Al Capone would have lived. The kind of place where Al Capone *did* live. After his infamous stint in prison for income tax evasion, Capone had retired to Miami. Prior to that, though, at the height of his power, he'd lived lavishly in Miami Beach, Florida.

The inherent contradiction in my father's stories frustrates me to this day.

At the farm, Mary Ann spoke with several people who said they remembered my father very well, but no one seemed to have any idea as to where he'd come from. James and Lillian had long since passed on, so the direct connection was unfortunately no longer valid. But, the farmhands were able to direct Mary Ann to other locals, some of whom were good friends of my father.

All of them remembered my father being warm and outgoing. He hadn't simply been a hired hand; he had been regarded as and treated as their son. They spoke of him being a hard worker around the farm, but also enjoying taking long drives into the country, while listening to the radio with the roof down in an early convertible he used to drive.

Of all the people Mary Ann spoke with during her trip to Illinois, perhaps none held as much potential as a spry, old gal named Betsy Sinclair. She had known my father very well. They'd gone to school together and hung out quite a bit. And, despite her advanced age, Betsy had little trouble recalling my father as a handsome man who was as kind and generous as any she'd ever known.

The way her eyes glistened when she spoke of my father, Mary Ann suspected they might have been a couple during their teen years.

"Were you close?" Mary Ann asked.

"Sure," said Betsy. "We were all close back then. It's a small town, after all."

"What about you and Bill? Did your relationship ever go beyond being just friends?"

But Betsy would not say whether they'd ever been a couple or not. Mary Ann figured that they were good friends who may have blurred the line between friends and lovers once or twice when they were hanging out, but that the relationship— for one reason or another—never fully blossomed into love. There was little doubt, however, that Betsy had great affection for my father and because of this affection, Mary Ann hoped her memories about what my father might have told her about his past would still be somewhat fresh.

Up until that point, when she had been speaking with the other locals who knew my father, Mary Ann had never broached the idea that he might be the son of Al Capone until she had exhausted every other tidbit of information. Her reasoning was sound: she had no desire to pollute whatever recollections they had of my father, especially since she was asking them to recall things from half a century or more before. With the injection of such a thought, they might well have imagined either that my father had said something, or someone had told them something, when in reality, such a thing had never happened at all.

Yet of all the people she spoke with, Mary Ann could not find one who could confirm or deny the idea that my father might have been Al Capone's son. Most of those she spoke with were able to recall only some aspects of their interactions with my father, and could offer very little in the way of concrete information other than what a good pal he'd been to hang around with.

It was only at the very end of her visit with Betsy Sinclair, when the two of them sat in rockers on the wraparound porch, sipping lemonade in the fading sunlight, that Mary Ann unleashed her mightiest question.

"We think William Knight might have been the son of Al Capone. What do you think of that?"

"What do I think?" Betsy smiled, took one last sip of her lemonade and said, "I think that sounds like something Bill would say."

Mary Ann then asked, "Did Bill ever lie, or make up stories?" Her answer to this question. "No—he was truthful."

And with that, Betsy got up, walked into her house and closed the door, leaving Mary Ann alone in the coming darkness.

Mary Ann and I both found Betsy's reaction unusual. Why wouldn't people talk about the possibility or even the fact that my father was Al Capone's son? Why would they prefer to keep this kind of information to themselves? It simply didn't make any sense. It wasn't as if Al could come back from the grave and kill them for leaking his precious secrets, was it?

Mary Ann located one other person on her trip to Illinois: Florence Horn. Flo's family lived across the street from the Buzick farm, but Flo was much younger than my father during his time there. Mary Ann got the distinct impression that Flo had had a mad crush on my father.

Flo's big brother, Delmar, had hung out with my father and was probably the closest to a best friend he might have had during his time on the farm. But Mary Ann couldn't pry much out of Flo and upon her return, I decided to call her myself.

"I think about your dad every day," she told me on the phone.

I decided to go for broke and ask her the penultimate question: "Was my dad the son of Al Capone?"

"I don't know anything." Her response came back at me fast, like it had been practiced for so long and said so often that it was now simply instinctive—a Pavlovian response to any question that mentioned Al Capone.

I pressed on. Flo suggested I call her brother, Delmar. "He might know something more than I do. He's in Texas now."

I had a three-way conversation with Delmar and his wife, via the phone. Delmar's wife spouted a great deal about how Delmar had thought my father was the greatest thing since sliced bread. "Delmar used to rave about your dad. It was always 'Bill this' or 'Bill that.'"

Delmar reminisced about the time my father and he had painted a windmill, hanging the buckets of paint on the windmill's fins in order to paint them. They'd used their hard-earned money for three gallons of gas, so they could go on a long drive. Delmar recalled last seeing my father in the early '60s, when my father was driving up to Illinois from Florida in a Cadillac convertible.

"Do you know where he came from?" I asked.

"We never asked him where he came from," said Delmar. "Didn't really think it was any of our business."

I sighed. "Delmar, I really want to know."

He paused. "Well, I know what you're talking about. But I don't think I can help you."

Florence Horn's name would continue to crop up during my investigations. Occasionally, during the 1940s, my father had actually listed her as his next of kin. This struck me as rather strange, and I would have loved to have followed up more with her about it. But, it followed certain logical patterns of how my father felt around that time—that later time, which I would soon learn more about.

There were periods during those years when he'd seemed adrift, and a kind friend from home, the girl next door perhaps, would have been a likely candidate for what meager largesse he had to offer, were he to have passed beyond this mortal coil. Flo spoke of my father sending her Sensen, a popular breath mint young people used at the time to cover up the smell of cigarettes or liquor. Apparently, it was considered rather exotic back in the Illinois farmlands. Ironically, it was also a favorite indulgence of Al Capone.

Mary Ann was forced to conclude that her trip to Illinois had resulted in us being no closer to the truth than when she'd been back in Boston, getting what little information she could from her extensive network of contacts. There seemed to be nowhere we could go in Illinois that would provide us with any concrete information. Our leads turned out to be worthless.

And any secrets Mary Ann and I had hoped to uncover on this particular leg of our bizarre journey seemed destined to remain just that: secrets. Whatever aspects of my father's past we knew had transpired during his time in Illinois, it was obvious to us that the people who could provide any more information—who could help us flesh out the details of my father's history—were simply not talking. Nor did they seem to have any desire to.

As time progressed, the big question of why people would choose not to share information with us—why they would prefer to keep things status quo—would rear its head over and over again.

ending.

NIGHT HI

U. S. GOVERNMENT PRINTING OF
AL SURVEY—FOLLOWING SHEET

AGE

e of hospital, ship, or station where survey is held)

APR 2 1946

OF CASE HISTORY

Illinois

At neuropsychiatric consultation a diagnosis of Con-
s made and he was transferred to this service.
tory reveals the patient to be an orphan who has n
of his parents. He was raised in a succession of rural,
ter homes. He was enuretic to the age of 12 and is a
from the age of 12 to 17 he lived on a farm in Illinois
ouple where he was treated for the first time not as a
son. He finished 2 years of high school. His 8 weeks in
r 10 months of service his foster father died and he was
duty to return and manage the farm. After a series of
idow regarding farm management and her affair with a
neighborhood, he was re-inducted in March of 1944 at

bizarre
Hysteri

ion revealed anxiety and a later markedly reduc
the examiner the impression that the patient was afraid
mental to himself. Wechsler-Bellevue examinat
with 24% intellectual deterioration. X-ray examination
d a small area of bone defect in the upper portion of

VI

IN THE NAVY

My father's time on the farm in rural Illinois drew to a close when he turned 17. One morning, after breakfast had been eaten and the chores had been finished, he hopped into his car and decided to drive himself into Chicago. Once there, he walked the streets until he located the Navy recruiting depot. With the old-time recruitment posters staring him in the face and the look of the men dressed smartly in their uniforms, my father promptly enlisted.

I imagine it must have seemed like the proper thing to do. With the rest of the world at war, a young man of my father's age undoubtedly saw himself as a necessary component in the machine that would prevent the evil Axis regimes from destroying the planet. At the same time, he most likely wondered whether he would be courageous enough to stand the extreme tests of combat. I imagine he felt like most young men: eager to prove themselves and with the nation at war, the higher calling of armed forces service would certainly outweigh any desire to stay in bucolic Illinois, shucking corn and planting crops on the farm.

But, there was a catch. My father, during the standard physical he received like every other volunteer, displayed some medical abnormalities, which, were it not a time of war, might have precluded him from serving in the armed forces.

My father had scarring on his eardrum. Medical records I later discovered revealed that he had informed the naval doctors that he'd had severe mastoid infections as a child, causing extraordinary ear pain and requiring hospitalization and treatment. He had told me as well about his being very, very sick when he was a young child. While he hadn't given me an exact age of occurrence, he'd said that it was pretty bad and that he'd almost died. He'd also told me that this near-death experience had touched him spiritually, that God must have been on his side with all the close calls he'd experienced during his life—many of which I was only later to uncover.

Stop.

Sonny Capone also had severe mastoid infections, causing his own ear problems, although Sonny's were alleged to have occurred when he was seven years old, which would have placed the malady in 1926, when my father would have been only one. The cause was said to be the untreated syphilis that killed his famous father, transmitted unknowingly from his father to his mother to him.

There were some additional questions that this raised as well. When, exactly, *did* Al Capone contract syphilis? While it was assumed that syphilis had caused Sonny Capone's ear problems, Capone was also said to have contracted the disease from a teenaged, blond girlfriend, well after his marriage to Mae. Around 1924 or 1925, to be exact.

My father, William Knight, was listed as having been born on July 14, 1925. If Sonny's mastoid infections were caused by Al's syphilis, Al would have to had contracted the disease prior to 1925. But, the 1925 syphilis timeline worked perfectly in possibly explaining my father's infections.

Sonny Capone was born out of wedlock. Mae and Al were married on December 30, 1918. Sonny was born on December 4, 1918. While Mae was actually two years Al's senior, all of Scarface's other girlfriends were young, quite young, almost always in their teens, some not even of legal age. Irene Maude Meis, the women on my father's birth certificate—whoever she was—would have been impregnated at the age of 18.

Al Capone took his son to the famed Johns Hopkins Hospital in Baltimore. It is said that he frantically grabbed a doctor by his white coat and said, "I'll give you $100,000 if you pull him through." Sonny lived. No one knew if Al ever paid up, but it was assumed that he had.

The Sonny Capone/William Knight parallels formed the greatest mysteries in my own mind. The most outlandish one may have been the one most solidly supported by my research—that *both* boys, at one time or another, were, in fact, Sonny Capone, and that Al, in his paranoia, hid his real son—my father, while posing as another boy—perhaps another of his actual offspring, perhaps maybe even a nephew— as Sonny—shades of Dumas' *The Man in the Iron Mask*.

This theory would only reveal itself to me as my research went on. Still, whenever they arose, the William/Sonny issues filled me with fear, anxiety and the excitement of discovery.

Sonny Capone was said to have recovered from his surgery with permanent hearing loss in one ear. My father, on the other hand, tested as having perfect hearing in both ears, both at his military induction as well as in subsequent check-ups years later, although he would continue to have medical problems regarding his ears—severe infections and the like—for the rest of his days.

The Sonny Capone mystery continued to loom large in my search. How did I know that Sonny had permanent hearing loss? He did everything in his power to avoid the public spotlight. His medical condition would have been spread to the world via relatively disinterested word-of-mouth. Partial hearing loss in only one ear was not front-page news, nor visibly noticeable.

My father had told me conflicting tales about his upbringing. At first, when I was quite young, he'd spoken of foster homes and the farm with the Buzicks. He'd then told his tale of changing the date on his birth certificate to 1925, so that he could serve his country during World War II.

I did not think this through at the time, nor would I have ever have disrespected my father's veracity. But, in 1942, when my father enlisted, his 1925 birth date would have made him 17 years old. Sonny Capone's birth date of December 4, 1918 would have made him 23 at the time my father enlisted— a perfectly acceptable age to enter the military, even had it not been wartime, when age restrictions were traditionally relaxed. Ironically, my father's claimed age of 17 was more controversial. It was, and remains, the very minimum age to enter the US Navy.

From September until October 1942, my father attended basic training at the US Naval Training Center in Great Lakes, Illinois. Upon graduation, he was transferred to Farragut, Idaho, where he entered and eventually graduated from Gunner's Mates Class "A" School. The 12 weeks he spent in Farragut brought him into contact with all manner of guns and cannons, skills he would need if he were to survive his assignment in the Pacific theater of operations.

For 10 months, my father served aboard a troop transport in the South Pacific. He saw firsthand some of the beach landings as the Allies hopscotched from island to island in a desperate bid to stop the Japanese steamroller from conquering the entire Pacific. As each island fell to the stalwart US Marines, my father no doubt wondered how much longer the war would continue, and what his role in it would be.

But at that point, nature suddenly intervened. Urgent news from the farm back home reached his ship and got him immediately dropped out of active duty. His foster father, James Buzick, who had been sick before, had suddenly died. My father was transferred back to the United States in order to attend the funeral and clear up any lingering family issues. It was also deemed necessary that he take over the managing of the family farm in the wake of his foster dad's death.

If there were one person not happy with my dad's return, it was his foster mother, Lillian. She had her own ideas about how the farm should be run and didn't see eye-to-eye with my father on anything. My father was of the opinion that more things needed mending in order to make the farm a sustainable and profitable enterprise. He wanted to start raising new crops, buying new machinery and generally attempting to upgrade the farm.

Lillian, however, liked things the way they were. She shrugged off my father's attempts to modernize and improve conditions. She also decided that the best way to mend her broken heart was to replace her dead husband with another man—a much younger man. She engaged in a spirited and somewhat crude love affair with a soldier from a neighboring town, who was far too many years her junior to ever be anything but a mere plaything.

I knew that this raucous display of affection infuriated my father, who was still deeply upset over the death of his foster father. My father had often told me that the Buzicks had treated him extremely well, and that he was indebted to them for their help during his childhood. I believe my father had felt strongly that if it hadn't been for James Buzick agreeing to take him into their home, he might not have survived to adulthood. My father's sadness was then compounded by his anger at seeing his foster mother cavorting about town with little more than a boy.

When his foster mother would return from her "outings" (as my father took to calling them) with this boy, he would ask her how she could do what she was doing when the memory of her husband was still so fresh. She had no answer for him except to say that what she did was her own business. Invariably, the heated arguments would conclude with them both storming off in a rage.

Things did not improve. The farm experienced a serious lack of business. Accounts fell short and Lillian continued traipsing about the countryside with different suitors in tow. More arguments ensued and things culminated with Lillian finally telling my father she didn't want him around the farm anymore. So, with little holding him to Illinois, and his sense of needing to serve his country still firmly entrenched in his soul, he re-enlisted in the Navy in March of 1944.

There was another mystery attached to this seemingly normal chain of human events, one that glared out at me from amongst the reams of papers that Mary Ann and her associates had gathered for me, along with much that I had uncovered on my own. Veterans Administration records codifying the event of my father's leave from service mention: "Out in June '43 because of political connections to return to farm of former foster father after the latter's death… Father Jim Busick [sic] died at 56 of heart trouble. Foster father from [ages] 12–17. No children. Wanted to adopt Knight and force him to take the name. [Knight] refused. Treated as a son. Only hit him twice."

Political connections? My father? The foster child of a poor farmer? *What* political connections? But Alphonse Capone had plenty of political connections, even at that stage in his life, when he was out of prison, but suffering from severe dementia from his untreated syphilis.

The part about taking on the Buzick name also struck me as revelatory. My father had never mentioned this to me, but psychologically, it seemed strange. The foster care system was unlike the adoption system. An adopted child was customarily taken in by some family from birth. A foster child usually yearned for similar treatment—to have a mom and dad and be surrounded by love, all of them having the same last name.

Why would my father, or any foster child for that matter, be so adamant about not giving up his last name if he did not really know or have any ties to his birth parents? I felt greater and greater confusion over these, the most banal factoids about my father. Who was he? Why did he think as he did? Why did he do what he did?

No doubt glad to have him back, the Navy immediately assigned my father to the USS Alhena in the Pacific theater of operations. The assignment was relatively uneventful, despite being in the midst of war. By then, it was reasonably clear that the Allies were winning the war both in Europe and in Asia. Japan and Germany were rocking back on their heels in the wake of some decisive victories. I wondered if my father felt that he might have missed a lot of the war while dealing with his ridiculous situation in rural Illinois.

If he were of that opinion, it changed on November 10, 1944. The night seemed serene, with the ships in my father's convoy docked in the placid waters of Manus Harbor, in the Admiralty Islands in the South Pacific.

Next to my father's ship, the Alhena, the USS Mount Hood was moored. The Mount Hood was being used as an ammunition ship, both receiving and delivering ammunition to other ships and fighters in the immediate vicinity. The Mount Hood's crew was working in all five of its vast holds when the next events occurred.

According to my father, who was on the deck of the Alhena, a sudden, sharp boom rang out and an almost perfect mushroom cloud—reminiscent of what would become the famous atomic bomb mushroom cloud—erupted. Immediately, secondary and tertiary explosions rang out, followed by scores more as the Mount Hood's ammo and munitions stores all exploded in rapid succession.

Fiery metal, chunks of debris, crew members and all manner of detritus rained down and out in all directions. The Mount Hood had been carrying roughly 3800 tons of ammunition at the time, including rockets, projectiles, bombs, fixed ammunition, smokeless powders, aerial bombs, torpedoes, depth charges, nose fuses and more. All of this material blew up in a truly spectacular fashion.

My father was knocked unconscious when white hot shards of steel fragmentation embedded themselves in his head, knocking him back and out of the gunner's position. The force of the shrapnel injury sent him sprawling over the deck, and he vaguely heard someone scream, "Corpsman!" just before everything went black.

He was unconscious for four hours while doctors worked on him. He sustained several severe lacerations across his face and scalp. The shrapnel caused a grotesque, compound, depressed fracture of his right frontal bone on his skull. Examining doctors also found depressed fractures of the nasal bones, and my father's septum appeared to have been crushed as a result of the battle injuries. He was transferred to a hospital ship, the USS Pinckney, three days later, when his injuries were deemed stable enough for him to be moved.

In the Mount Hood explosion, 45 sailors had been killed and 371 injured, my father being just one of them. He recalled seeing horribly wounded men all around him in the sick bay while doctors had tried to triage them as best they could. The floor had run slick with the red blood of the injured and dying. My father realized how unbelievably lucky he had been to survive such a terrible explosion. Coming face-to-face with his mortality may have made him seriously reconsider whether he wanted to stay in the Navy at all.

While he was being treated, my father complained of headaches occurring on the right side of his head. He also routinely stated that he had accompanying dizzy spells and had experienced amnesia—entire blocks of time where snippets of conversation vanished. The chief medical officer aboard the Pinckney wrote in my father's medical records that as a result of the depressed fracture, my father might have even been at risk for developing epilepsy. He urged further evaluation, given the nature of his injuries. And on December 17, the doctor wrote that my father would require more than 120 days of hospitalization. He further suggested that my father was unfit for duty outside the US.

Logically, the Navy ran batteries of tests on him, but the results came back as negative for any type of neurological damage. My father's physical injuries also continued to heal well. As such, he returned to active duty on February 6, 1945.

For three months thereafter, he served on an LCI (landing craft infantry) stationed in the Philippines. Life aboard the LCI was largely uneventful—most of the major combat operations were north of the Philippines, and my father spent his time aboard ship enveloped in boredom.

Naval   USS TEMPT[...]

Mr. William George Knight
162 20 89 Avenue
Apt 4A
Jamaica, New York

Mar 44 Reenl   USNR V6, [...]
Mar 44 RepAD&T   NTS Farra[...]
Apr 44 CR   S2
Chicago, Ill. As   S1
Apr 46 Dis

Dear Mr. Knight:

In compliance with your desirable [...]
is furnished the complete transcrip[...]
Naval service:

cords show you served on board the fo[...]

3 Sep 1942 Enl in the USNR as AS
            Ill., to serve for a p[...]
            active duty, T & R [...]
15 Oct 1942 T to Section Base, [...]
[..] 1942   R at RS, New York, N.[...]
28 Oct 1942 T to U.S.S. TEMPRESS
3 Nov 1942 R in U.S.S TEMPRESS.
[...]   CR to S2c.
[...]   [Dis]charged with an Hon[...]
3 Mar 1944 Reenlisted in the USNR
            serve for a period of
            and T to NTS, Farragut
[..] Mar 1944 R at NTS, Farragut, [...]
17 [..] 1944 CR to S2[c]
[..] [..] 1944 T to RecBks, Shoemaker
25 Sep 1944 T & R in U.S.S. ALHE[...]
10 Nov 1944 T & R in Base Hospital
14 Nov 1944 T to U.S.S. PINKNEY
19 Nov 1944 R at Fleet Hospital [...]
17 Dec 1944 T to a Naval Hospital
11 Jan 1945 R at USNH, Great Lake[...]
5 Feb 1945 T to RecBks, Shoemake[...]
13 Feb 1945 R in RecBks, Shoemak[...]
21 Mar 1945 T & R at RecShip, Sa[...]
17 Apr 1945 T to ComAdCom[...]
[..] Jun 1945 R in U.S.S. LCI[...]
1 Aug 1945 [...]
1 Sep 1945 T & R at Fleet Hospi[...]
19 Sep 1945 T to nearest USNH in
9 Oct 1945 R in USNH, Seattle, W[...]

ssels
[Con]ditions,
S TEMPRESS
S SALEM (Transport)
S PINKNEY (Transport [...])
S LCI(L) 1032

Chicago, July 1946, Chicago, Illinois
direction of Chief of Naval Personnel
daho

St. Albans, L. I. N[...]

VII

THE SAFEST PLACE TO HIDE?

In July of 1945, my father started experiencing persistent headaches, dizziness, and a growing incidence of clumsiness. He apparently told the doctors that while onboard the LCI he was assigned to, he "slipped down more hatches than [he] walked down." The doctor conducted a thorough examination, especially in light of my father's rather recent medical injuries.

Results of the battery of tests showed that my father had gross motor problems, hesitant speech and slight hand-eye coordination issues. He was released with an aspirin regimen, only to return frequently to sick call with similar complaints. This back-and-forth continued for several months.

By September 1945, my father's complaints had worsened; frequent, debilitating headaches plagued him. He was excitable and nervous, and severe dizziness rendered him almost invalid.

His walking gait suffered to the point that he developed a severe limp in his right leg.

The ship's doctors examined him as extensively as they could, given the confines of a naval ship, but could not determine anything was wrong with him aside from some vague imperfections on basic hand-eye coordination tests. Realizing that my father's condition might be more serious than they were able to evaluate, especially since the symptoms seemed to be worsening, they evacuated him to the States aboard a hospital ship.

My father returned to the United States and was immediately admitted to the US Naval Hospital in Seattle, Washington, on October 9, 1945. Again, all tests and examinations showed nothing abnormal. My father continued to complain of severe headaches, dizziness and difficulty walking. The general staff at USNH Seattle decided the best thing to do would be to transfer him to another hospital. My father was transferred to the US Naval Hospital in Oakland, California.

Upon his admittance, my father continued to complain about headaches, dizziness and a strange gait to his walk. All of these factors were noted by attending physicians. As a result of what medical officers had written on his last duty ship, my father underwent an electroencephalogram, to rule out psycho-motor problems. Doctors also started considering whether his ailments and complaints might have originated from a neurological perspective, rather than as a result of lingering and previously unknown physical problems. All of these tests came back as negative for anything serious.

The medical staff next decided to administer other neurological evaluations, including a series of psychiatric tests designed to explore further into my father's mind. Results obtained after the Rorschach evaluation indicated that my father had a tremendous amount of anxiety. He was classified as neurotic and the physicians believed he seemed concerned about possibly revealing something that might prove detrimental to himself.

While it was noted that he was an agreeable sort—cooperative, and sometimes pleasant—doctors were quick to point out that my father seemed to have an inordinate amount of repressed hostility, especially toward people he believed had taken advantage of him at some point. He also seemed to believe that no one would ever think he was a real citizen of the United States, leading him to state that he would get a "Yankee pin and wear it on my back."

My father had no accent that might make people suspect him as being an immigrant. Furthermore, the man I'd known as my father had not been brimming with anxiety. Far from the case, he had been the eye in the center of our ongoing family storm, *i.e.*, my mother. He had always been the port of safe passage for my sister and me.

Additionally, despite the discoveries I made after my father died, while alive, he'd never carried himself as a man with secrets. But indeed, he now appeared to have had many, some of them critically serious. While some men might have lived a life of disquietude due to repressed confidences, he'd appeared to all as rather placid, relaxed and at peace with himself. Had the Navy so cowed him that he'd felt he could not keep up some charade he'd been leading, or in which he'd been complicit?

And what of the repressed anger and resentment his

doctors felt they'd discovered? Again, the man I'd known was not without faults, but suppressed rage or loathing was not at all one of them. These had been far more the traits of my mother, who had seemed angry at the world for having dealt her a hand of cards she'd reviled.

Doctors continued to administer a wide array of tests, reexamining my father's head wound and the resulting scars. None of his previous physical ailments showed any signs of being infected, or of otherwise developing complications that might have accounted for his behavior and symptoms.

Simultaneously, they calculated his IQ as being 94, with a 24 percent intellectual deterioration. Further mental evaluations revealed "an immature, suspicious, wary individual of average intelligence and poor insight." All of those factors coincided nicely with what the medical officers had suspected all along—that my father was suffering due to head trauma, brought on as a result of his injuries in the wake of the Mount Hood disaster.

But a discovery in September of 1945 cast new light on my father's condition. Inexplicably, he was found wearing a length of rubber tubing like a tourniquet on his upper right arm. The pressure caused by this tubing would certainly have contributed to the wide spectrum of ailments he'd complained about. My father later admitted that he had been wearing this device frequently throughout many of the preceding months. With the tubing removed, he completely recovered from his complaints. His normal walking gait returned and all other symptoms disappeared after the tubing was discarded.

With the physical ailments seemingly cured, doctors turned their attention to the reasons why my father would concoct such a strange malady. In the wake of the discovery of his fabrication, my father admitted that he'd been worried about his financial well-being, and how he would return to normal society after serving in the war. For those reasons, he'd decided to fabricate the appearance of being sick in order to remain "safely" hospitalized.

Medical officers wrote a lengthy report documenting my father's behavior and actions. They admitted that due to his service on a variety of vessels and also his proximity to wounded sailors after the Mount Hood explosion, my father had seen enough patients classified as hemiplegics to understand how to imitate their symptoms. Several doctors noted that my father seemed to truly enjoy and relish all the attention being paid to him—both by the staffs of the hospitals he had been sent to and the various charity organizations that inevitably fawned over wounded servicemen.

Given my father's foster background and the fact that he had done no thinking about what his future might hold since the Buzick farm had been sold off by his foster mother, his thirst for attention was seen as somewhat normal. His mental alertness was also deemed as out of character for a hemiplegic; genuine patients would have pleaded for treatment while my father had apparently offered one of the doctors a "clock if you can cure me." (Obviously, he did not have access to a $100,000 cash bribe.)

Despite their obvious displeasure with my father for fabricating his illness and all his physical complaints after his head injury, they were quick to note that anyone who had been injured in a similar manner might have exhibited the same tendencies. The USS Mount Hood incident was deemed tragic enough to have witnessed, let alone been injured by, to lead someone potentially to pretend that they were more seriously ill than they actually were.

After counseling my father further, the team of doctors noted that he realized his mistakes and seemed sorry for the trouble he had caused, as well as for the time he had wasted. Medical staff assigned to his case submitted a lengthy report that concluded that he presented no danger to society, and was therefore able to be released into his own care. The medical team also did not believe he would end up a public charge on welfare and as such, no disciplinary action was to be pursued. My father, realizing that he might get himself into trouble if he did so, wisely chose to not rebut their findings, and accepted their evaluations with aplomb.

To say that I was aghast at reading these reports would be putting it mildly. They accused my father of being, for lack of a better word, a hypochondriac, complete with the insatiable need for attention. Again, nothing could be further from the truth.

A quick analysis: my father had been in a horrific wartime accident and had received a fractured skull. That, combined with the momentum of this particular war itself, made it highly illogical for him or any man to believe sincerely that he would be sent back to frontline duty, dodging bullets and bombs, fearing for his life.

He was described, though, as being of relatively simple mind and intellect and, according to the Navy, would perhaps not have been in possession of the mental faculties to arrive at that conclusion himself. Were this also true, I failed to understand how his intellect could have improved as much as it had in his later years, once he had been in my life. The findings simply did not fit the real man.

Unless the man was faking it. But faking what, exactly? And why?

The Navy's simple explanations, done through the prism of its institutional viewpoint and assumedly in great rapidity, due to its more obvious priorities of winning a major war, appeared to me to be quite inadequate and, in fact, dead wrong.

To analyze further, a man was injured in combat; he wanted to come home. He did not wish to see more combat. But my father was never noted as requesting or demanding transport home, and disengagement from the service. Quite the opposite.

The Navy noted the traits of a man reluctant to return home for fear of starting a new life. This fear was realistic, one illuminated marvelously in two of the greatest war films ever made: *The Best Years of Our Lives* and *The Deer Hunter*.

But, these two observations contradict. A man afraid of returning home would not pretend that his very real injuries were worse than they were. He would not tie a tourniquet on his arm to exacerbate his existing injuries, unless his fear of returning stateside had to do with embarrassment at his diminished physical state.

Which brought up a third theory, one which the naval doctors would not have dreamed to imagine: he had been hiding out in the Navy. Not avoiding the re-entry into the basic institution of American freedom and adulthood, full of responsibilities and individual choices, but perhaps afraid of facing a far more unique welcome: the wrong end of a tommy gun or a birth father, crazed yet knowing that the end of his life was near. Or both.

It was well noted in American crime lore that Al Capone was never sentenced to prison for his murders, his rackets, or any of the other vicious, inhumane crimes he committed against individuals and against the state. He was finally brought down by Al Alcini, the self-promoting Eliot Ness and his Untouchables, and IRS agent Frank Wilson, for the white collar crime of income tax evasion.

On October 17, 1931, Big Al Capone was sentenced to 11 years in federal prison. On May 4, 1932, he began serving his sentence in the Atlanta Federal Penitentiary. This was not a roaring success for those who wished to see the big man broken down. In Atlanta, Capone was treated like royalty: he flaunted his power, was given unfettered access to the warden, and was said to have maintained large caches of cash in his cell, in order to "tip" the guards as if they were waiters in a swank Chicago bistro.

When word of this behavior sprang forth in August of 1934, Attorney General Homer Cummings and Sanford Bates, head of federal prisons, unceremoniously put Scarface on a prison railroad car to a ferry port, to be taken to that most disheartening of penal journeys: Alcatraz, America's Devil's Island.

Alcatraz and its denizens treated Big Al not as the Boss of Bosses, but simply as AZ-85, his official prison number. And Al did not like it one bit. But in the end, it was Capone who was broken, not the system. It certainly did not help that Capone, while still a man in the prime of life—he had been only 35 years old when he'd arrived at Alcatraz—began his final downward physical and mental spiral due to untreated syphilis, a disease he had been carrying for years.

There were many theories as to why this man, this powerful, intimidating figure, allowed himself to go untreated for what is today a very treatable disease. Penicillin, syphilis' cure, had only been discovered in 1928. It had not been used successfully to treat human patients until 1942. It had soon rushed in to help Allied soldiers in World War II, and it could be hypothesized that this discovery was as important to victory as a major weapon in the Allies' efforts to slay the Axis powers of Hitler's Germany and Tojo's Japan.

By 1938, Al Capone was so riddled with syphilis that he was transferred to Terminal Island Prison in Southern California, and finally to Baltimore State Mental Institution, to serve out the remainder of his sentence. He was finally released in 1939.

From November of 1939 to January of 1947, Capone lived in his Palm Beach mansion, a doddering, sick shell of his former self. His mind had so deteriorated that it was assessed that he had the mental capacity of a 13-year-old at best. He was known to wander outside clad in only his pajamas, ranting and raving, while embarrassed bodyguards tended to his needs.

Capone's disease had been left untreated for too long. Furthermore, while America remained at war, literally all supplies of penicillin were rationed to US troops. Despite his power and influence, there was little that Big Al or his gang could do to save him.

Could it have been that my father had known by that time that he was Al Capone's son? In such a situation, had he been seeking the protection of the US Navy?

While Capone had been incarcerated, his control on

Chicago had begun to crumble. Frank "The Enforcer" Nitti, Al's selected heir apparent, could not control the gang's underlings as had Capone. Fragmentation ensued. Things had gotten so bad that on March 19, 1943, Nitti had shot himself to death.

Nitti had been succeeded by Paul "The Waiter" Ricca, whose betrayal of Nitti had broken The Enforcer's spirit and led to his decision to end his own life. Soon thereafter, Ricca had been sent to prison, as federal agents had gotten far more savvy in their pursuit of major Mafia figures, particularly those in and around Chicago.

Finally, Tony "Big Tuna" Accardo, one of the last of Capone's major personal henchmen, had taken over the gang. Accardo may have been the smartest of them all, keeping as low a profile as possible, in stark contrast to Capone himself. No publicists or front-page pictures for The Big Tuna, who'd stayed on the scene until he'd died of natural causes in 1992, without having ever spent a night in jail.

One would question how a Capone heir would have fared in wake of this shifting of criminal power. Capone's brothers, most of whom were involved with Big Al's criminal operation, were considered either physically or mentally too weak to ever keep the power within the Capone family name. They all gradually evolved into smalltime jobs and businesses, set up for them by Al's largesse. There they remained, never attempting a power grab, even in times of a leadership vacuum.

The man known as Sonny Capone? During Al's stint in Atlanta and later Alcatraz, Sonny and Mae had visited him with great frequency. In 1937, Sonny entered the University of Notre Dame, the leading Catholic college in America.

He lasted one year before transferring to the University of Miami, where he graduated in 1941, having studied business administration.

On New Year's Eve, 1941, Sonny married Diana Ruth Casey, his high school sweetheart, and opened a flower shop in Miami, not far from his father's estate. He eventually floated in and out of sight, taking on relatively menial jobs and occupations while producing four heirs of his own. As I mentioned before, he eventually changed his name to simply Albert Francis, his first and middle names, in a further attempt to achieve anonymity.

Could my father have had a realistic fear for his safety in light of Al Capone's diminishing influence? If he had known by 1945 that Capone was indeed his father, this would have been a very realistic possibility.

Another theory emerged: assuming again that he'd known by 1945 that Al Capone was his father, and that his father was a sick, deranged man, would my father have wanted to be pulled into the man's still considerable vortex? I was only led to believe by my father himself that there had been a brief period wherein he'd shared time, perhaps, with the man—during his childhood, shortly prior to his turning up on the Buzick farm, when he'd claimed to have lived in a mansion in Florida.

His years from the Buzick farm forward appeared to be fairly well accounted for in terms of lack of personal, physical contact with the Boss of Bosses. Would a young man in that situation want to attempt to bond with a madman murderer? Or would he have tried to avoid any possible physical contact, such as by remaining bound to the service?

My father was finally disengaged from active duty and from the Naval Reserves with an honorable discharge on April 30, 1946, in St. Albans, Long Island, New York. In later years, he would often remark that he was proud of the time he had served his country, especially since it had been during wartime. I imagined that he, like most veterans, had enjoyed knowing they had contributed—even in some small way—to protecting the American way of life.

My father's personal journey was moving into a new area—one wherein he would be forced out into the real world, the world of a private citizen with no commanding officer to wake him in the morning or order his activities during the day. He had to find a job, a place to live, and to make a life for himself—alone, no longer with ties to his late, beloved foster father, Jim Buzick, or his stepmother, Lillian. But the question in my mind remained: was there a benevolent angel or a malevolent devil watching over him?

Photo taken by my father in the early 1950's of a tanker he was about to board.

VIII

THE STRANGE, POST-WAR YEARS

On April 30, 1946, my father, William Knight, Jr., was officially disengaged from the US Navy via an honorable discharge. His journeys over the next several years would perplex me at every turn.

Only one week after leaving the Navy, he entered navigation school at the Merchant Marine Academy in King's Point, New York. The academy was in its infancy, having only been dedicated and declared open by President Franklin Delano Roosevelt in September of 1943. While today it stands as a traditional four-year college program, during World War II and shortly thereafter, it was used to fill the emergency needs of a country at war, desperately in need of men with training in navigation, ship's administration, electrical and mechanical systems, and customs. The conversion to a four-year service academy ála West Point or Annapolis began in 1948, after my father had left.

I find it curious that a man who had hidden out in the Navy, and who had even faked battlefield injuries or intentionally exacerbated such injuries, would immediately dash back into a military environment. I also questioned where he got the money for such adventures, but the G.I. Bill was in place since 1944 and certainly would have helped thousands of servicemen like my father with their educational needs.

This, though, did bring up another remembrance from my more recent past, one wherein my mother was spouting off about my father. My mother made no secret of the fact that she assumed that my father was the son of Al Capone. I found this strange, as she certainly never mentioned any such thing while my father had still been alive; only upon my raising the issue long after his passing did she answer in the affirmative to the question, "Was Dad Al Capone's son?"

Her casualness about the subject struck me as odd, as if I had asked her, "Were Dad's eyes brown?" To support her claim—as I was certainly not about to take such a revelation at face value from a woman I had little reason to trust or believe—she mentioned that Al Capone had paid for my father's wartime schooling at an academy in Madison, Wisconsin.

I tracked down the records and yes, my father had indeed attended a military training school in Wisconsin during his first stint in the Navy, prior to taking leave to go back and attempt to run the Buzick farm. He had also done so prior to the passage of the G.I. Bill. But, the academy was a purely military school, where he was trained in weaponry and marksmanship. Would an America at war charge one of its enlisted men to attend such a school, G.I. Bill or no G.I. Bill? I highly doubt it. Yet, there was another red herring thrown in my path and I had to pick it up and examine it with a jaundiced eye.

Ralph "Bottles" Capone, Al's older brother, also lived in Wisconsin for a time. Ralph was not a bright man, but was the person Al trusted most. Al's temper was infamous, and it was said that Ralph was the only person with the ability to calm him down.

Ironically, Ralph spent time in prison on charges of tax evasion prior to Big Al's conviction on the same charge. One would think that Scarface would have seen it all coming. The IRS actually considered their prosecution of Ralph to be a test case before proceeding forward with their actions against Al.

Ralph had a son named Ralphie (Ralph, Jr.), who would have been about the same age as the man known as Sonny Capone. Ralph was born in 1917, Sonny in 1919, my father—allegedly—in 1925, depending upon whether one believed his birth certificate or his oral claims to the contrary. I looked at pictures of Sonny Capone and most of them from his childhood and young adulthood looked nothing like my father. Fright-eningly enough, they looked a lot like me. On the other hand, pictures of Ralphie, Al's nephew, looked extraordinarily like my father. Ralphie committed suicide in 1950, at the age of 33.

Documentation would later track that my father did not fully complete his navigational training, complaining of reverberations from his war injuries—severe headaches, black outs and nausea. Nonetheless, he found his way back onto a ship, working aboard a merchant vessel, the SS Horizon, which docked out of Newcastle on Tyne, England. Peace had only recently been achieved against the Nazis, in May of 1945, and there appeared to be a booming need for the revitalization of regular merchant shipping services between Europe and the Western Hemisphere.

Funny, but a father would usually tell his son about such exotic trips abroad. Yet my father, in the 13 years I knew him, never specifically mentioned serving on a ship out of England during peacetime, or of time spent in England at all. He always appeared to be a well-traveled man, but so many of the specifics—the tales a father would spin for his only son— were absent from my life.

The more I read about his excursions, years after he died, the more perturbed I became. My sister and I had been robbed of so much—so much time potentially spent in his loving presence, listening to the stories people in the twilight of their years love to tell. Not only was I finding secrets and mysteries, but even the pedestrian and the banal irked and saddened me.

My father stepped off the SS Horizon for the final time in Baltimore, Maryland, on January 27, 1948. Less than two weeks later, on February 9, he married Barbara McLeran Adams in Lowndes County, Georgia.

What?!

My father had mentioned to my sister and I that he had married before. He'd said that his first wife had been a Florida socialite. The mental picture was a pretty one: a glammed-up Hollywood scene that stood in stark contrast to the truck driving, overall and fedora wearing, older man who helped raise me. But this socialite had no name; I knew of no Barbara. Furthermore, he'd explained to us that this first wife had died young, of cancer. Barbara Adams Knight did no such thing.

Any erudite person would be drawn immediately to the

dates. Stepping off of a merchant ship one day, married 13 days later and four states further south. How did such a thing come to happen?

My father's only other mention of romance had been a tale of having had a Filipino girlfriend during his time in the Navy, during the war. That affair had ended, he'd told us, when she'd plunged off a mountaintop to her death, when he'd declined to marry her. This was a dramatic, romantic vision as well, as visually dynamic as the yarn about the Florida socialite who'd died young and beautiful, a victim of incurable cancer.

Was my father a pathological liar?

One could certainly make that accusation of the teller of such fables. I would prefer to believe, through my rose-colored glasses of affection, that they were more the fairy tales a loving parent would tell to his progeny as they sat aglow with antici-pation at his feet. But, the cynicism of my adulthood looked for more plausible answers, ones more in line with the pattern all those fallacies were forming, together as parts of a whole.

Putting aside the brokenhearted native Filipino girl, Barbara Adams was an enigma. What I'd come to know about her was this: she'd resided in Tampa, Florida, with her parents, and she and my father had continued to list her parents' Tampa address as their own for the duration of their marriage. They'd owned no place of their own in Florida. Barbara's father had been the local sheriff, a somewhat ironic factoid.

Yet my father was somehow a traveling man. In July of 1948, in correspondence with the Veterans Administration, he gave his home address as being in care of a Mr. Sharp in Rego Park, Long Island, New York.

Mr. Sharp was still alive. By then, my personal sleuthing skills had become near professional in quality. But, like so many people I tracked down in my quest for truth and closure, Mr. Sharp was not simply taken aback by my entry into his life; he was downright angry as hell.

After quizzing me with great acrimony as to how I'd found him, I finally snuck in the key purpose of my call. "Did you know a man named William Knight?"

"I don't know anyone named William Knight." Slam!

If this exchange had been in person and his door had just been slammed in my face, I would have still been there, mangled foot in the doorway, knocking once again.

Ring! "Could it be that you may have run a boarding house or rented rooms at some time in your life? I'm trying to figure out why he was having his mail forwarded to you."

Slam!

This continued through a handful more telephone hang-ups, as I was developing a thick skin to rejection. An inquisitive mind regarding it as well. If someone called me out of the blue and asked me if I knew someone, even if I were quite indisposed at the time, I would, at worst, be a bit curt and dismissive, but certainly not as ferociously angry as many of the people who had been associated with my father were. I would even volunteer to call them back if there seemed at all a chance that I might know who they were talking about. That is, if I weren't participating in a conspiracy of silence. If I didn't have something to hide.

Meanwhile, only five days after his wedding to Barbara Adams, my father began taking classes at Brewster Vocational

School in Tampa, in order to study accounting. A short honey-moon following a short courtship, it would seem.

Now, there were very logical solutions to the obvious questions this all presented. Perhaps my father had met Barbara sometime while on leave, then corresponded with her, fallen in love and, once off the Horizon, raced down south to take her as his bride. It sounded plausible; it sounded romantic. To me, it just didn't sound right.

I had known for years that my own parents' marriage had been an arranged one. I would later discover that my father had a second wife, after his marriage to Barbara ended in divorce. That courtship, too, had been extraordinarily short. A pattern, perhaps? And if so…why?

By February of 1948, Al Capone had been dead for slightly over a year. His widow, Mae, still lived in their Florida mansion. The man known as Sonny Capone was keeping a very low profile and was said to be living not far from Al's estate. Ralph Capone had also taken up semipermanent residence in the Sunshine State. And then, my father was married and living in Florida. There were 48 states in the union. What were the chances?

I could conjecture many things from this all-in-the-family-in-Florida period. Was my father brought into the fold somewhat after insane, syphilitic Al had died? Or was he boldly peeking in the window, so to speak, getting close to the life he could have had but did not for one reason or another? I may never have known. He was dead and, much to my chagrin, no one else was talking.

This much I did know. My father started having severe

headaches again and some physical symptoms reminiscent of his ailments while in service. Being a veteran, he sought the medical advice of the Veterans Administration, beginning on February 24, 1948. All physical examinations revealed nothing wrong, but less than a month later, he was started on a steady prescription of Phenobarbital, a barbiturate frequently used as an anticonvulsive and/or a sedative. The prescription was refilled each month thereafter, despite there being no change in my father's physical condition. As a result, the Veterans Administration concluded that he should receive disability compensation for his injuries received during his service.

It seemed apparent that my father might have taken advantage of the VA system to some extent. On the surface, he seemed perfectly healthy, and yet in his correspondence with the VA, there was a clear and marked tendency for his writing to devolve into gibberish. He requested numerous examinations and made numerous appeals to the doctors for help with his condition.

As a result of his condition, the Veterans Administration concluded that my father would receive compensation at a 30 percent rate, rather than the 50 percent rate he sought. A 100 percent rating would indicate the medical opinion that a man was completely incapacitated and totally unable to work. These smaller increments indicated a diminished physical or mental capacity, signifying the ability to work somewhat, but not able to earn as much as if a man were in a perfectly healthy condition.

My father appeared before the St. Petersburg, Florida, Veterans Administration Passa-Grille Regional Office on September 1, 1948, along with his lawyer, Mr. Doncaster, to appeal the 30 percent rating. After a brief interview, during which my father answered many questions about the blackouts he'd been experiencing that resulted in him missing classes in accounting at the local vocational school, the board adjourned to consider his appeal.

They quickly returned, and as a result of a medical evaluation conducted in June of 1948, they concluded that the 30 percent compensation rate offered was suitable for what my father was experiencing. The case was referred to the VA Board of Appeals. I believed that they upheld the first board's judgment.

My father's marriage to Barbara Adams Knight seemed to be on the rocks almost from the start—not unusual, one might suspect, for a couple united after only a nine-day courtship.

In statements to a VA medical examiner during psychological testing, Dad mentioned Barbara as being "under doctor's orders at all times." For what? When asked about their sex life, he responded by saying, "If things go wrong, I am usually to blame. She is very nervous." It was chivalrous of him to take the rap for their bedroom problems, and describing her as nervous during their attempts at lovemaking might not be too much of a stretch for a couple who were literal strangers to one another.

He went on to say, under subsequent questioning, that his wife Barbara was "unable to work." Again, no reason given, just the inference that Barbara was somehow a sickly or unstable person.

The sexual *coup de gras* finally came in the form of a typed letter from my father to the VA, again begging for enhanced

disability benefits, wherein he said, almost entirely incoher-
ently, "My wife want to have children. I went to a doctor and
he run some test on me and found out that I am impotency
unable to produce seaman [sic] in which make children... This
is and may break up my home."

There were two observations I made from this particular
letter. One, it appeared to be from a man who was either
stupid, crazy or trying to demonstrate diminished mental
capacity. The other observation was something even the VA
did not know, but I did: my father did not type.

Someone else typed the letter. Who? Barbara? Perhaps.
But, other parts of the letter disparaged her as well, so it was
doubtful to be her handiwork.

These letters, as well as actual medical reports from the
days of his marriage to Barbara Adams, painted a picture of
either a very badly injured man who never fully recovered from
his wartime head trauma, or a hypochondriac beggar. Neither
could be further from the man I knew. Yes, a child will always
place a parent upon a pedestal, although my estimation of my
mother would be a stark exception. But, throughout this
process of searching for answers, I wracked my brain to
remember everything about my father in a true and honest
light.

My father was often sick and unwell, but not with the
complaints noted in his naval records. He almost perpetually
ran a fever, always had a cough and would sweat constantly.
But, never did he complain of blackouts, headaches or any
of the maladies described in those VA medical reports done
in the decade after his departure from the US Navy. Neither
was he a hypochondriac, always complaining of *something*.

Hypochondriacs seek attention. My father did not.

As to the begging, this brought up yet another issue. My father, during my days, was always a hardworking man and did not ever preach the sermon of "screw over they neighbor." His hand was never out, except to help his fellow man, never asking for alms for his own needs. Could he have been going through a tough period financially? Perhaps. But, the G.I. Bill also provided the 52-20 Clause, which provided servicemen $20 per week for 52 weeks a year, while they were out of work and seeking employment. It was said that less than 20 percent of that money was ever dispersed by the US government because employment was so easy to come by during those first few years in post-WWII America.

My father appeared to have been living under his in-laws' roof and he and Barbara had no children. Between his disability pension, his lack of bills and the 52-20 money available to him, there was little logical reason for him to try to scam the VA system for more than he deserved.

But, this was still a man who had tied a tourniquet on his arm in order to exacerbate his real wartime injuries. While my theory that he was avoiding leaving the ship or the Naval hospital so as to avoid Capone's rivals or even the big boss himself, neither of these motivations would explain my father's behaviors in the late '40s and early '50s.

Putting aside disparaging views of the man my father might have been at the time—as he certainly displayed none of those traits later in life—I can hypothesize that perhaps he was creating a paper trail for himself, a byway of breadcrumbs to keep him on record somehow, somewhere.

Again, my father seemed to travel a lot, far more than I had ever been led to believe. Much of his correspondence with the VA came from New York addresses. In later years, I also found significant caches of foreign money in my father's possession. These were not the single dollar bills a collector might have, but great wads of exotic currency. Where did he get it? When did he get it? I had no idea.

Why would my father have wished to keep up these trail markings with the federal government? Could it have been that he was under investigation, as had been Capone and his entire extended family? In the years immediately proceeding, during, and even after the death of Big Al, the Capones were harassed constantly by the feds. Ralph "Bottles" Capone was brought before the famed Kefauver Committee in Washington, one of the first major congressional investigations into this thing that became known as the Mafia. It was shortly thereafter that his son, Ralphie, committed suicide.

Even Al's only non-criminal brother, Vincenzo, better known as James, was dragged into a federal courtroom to testify during the second tax evasion trial of brother Ralph. John Capone was put before the Kefauver Committee. Brother Albert, so desirous of the straight life after a few years spent with brother Alphonse, changed his last name in 1942 to Rayola—an Americanization of his mother's maiden name, Raiola—in order to drop out of sight.

The actions of the brothers Capone, though, almost contradicted this theory. Many of them were doing whatever they could to *not be* accounted for by the federal government. My father was doing quite the opposite.

Trouble in marital paradise continued for William and

Barbara Knight. Her parents especially did not seem thrilled that their only daughter had taken up with an incapacitated man like my father. But what eventually made them all the more upset was how what my father claimed about his health seemed to be at odds with the reality of his situation.

Specifically, my father used to take frequent trips north from Florida, where he was living at the time, to New York City. And yet, he was supposedly unemployed and seemingly unable to support a wife and family.

During that time, there remained a Capone presence in New York, the place of the family's settling after emigrating from Italy, yet my father had always only listed Illinois as the place of his personal roots, aside from the tales of his short time spent in a Florida mansion. I wondered how New York fit into his life, why he was drawn there, and how he paid for such travel at a time when he was crying poverty.

My father continued to receive his disability compensation from the Veterans Administration, yet took jobs here and there, during which time he never seemed to exhibit the afflictions he claimed prevented him from finding full-time work.

Barbara's parents probably felt that my father was using the military public assistance system to his advantage. He would get fixed money from the VA each month and then supplement it with the money he earned from working odd jobs. Angry and worried, Barbara's parents wrote a letter to the Veterans Administration, informing them that my father seemed to be conning the system. They stressed the importance of confidentiality; they wanted to make sure that my father never discovered that they had written the letter blowing the whistle on his questionable activities.

As a result, the VA decided to cancel my father's disability checks. I had a letter dated December 26, 1952, which noted the great concern my father had over this decision. He wrote to the Veterans Administration in St. Petersburg, Florida, imploring them to reconsider their decision.

The VA had apparently scheduled him for yet another series of medical tests, to determine if his physical condition actually existed at all, but when it appeared that my father would be unable to get down to their facility in time to take the tests, they simply decided to cancel the disability benefits. My father's letter stated that he would be down there to take the tests, and how badly he wanted to get things squared away.

My father's typewritten letter (from my non-typing father) also noted the following: "I hope you will be able to continue my disability compensation until the end of the year. My wife is also in bad health and paying for her and my doctor's bills was taking all of my check and some beside. I promise I will be there to take this physical examination any time after the 1st of February. And if I get into Tampa sooner I will drop over and see you. As I stated before I don't get my letter right away. Please allow me time to receive them."

It seems apparent that the Veterans Administration sent several letters to my father, suggesting that he come in to take some tests, to determine his candidacy for continued disability compensation. Whether deliberate or simply a victim of the postal system's incompetence, my father apparently had the habit of responding too late to letters. It certainly did not help that he was constantly changing his mailing address. Yet, Barbara's family in Tampa never moved during that time and as he and Barbara were still married, it would seem perfectly logical that if all correspondence were sent to that address, he would get them eventually. But logic was a game of diminishing returns in this investigation.

Taking in concert the letter from Barbara Adams Knight's parents, and the lengthy medical evaluations that suggested my father had lingering neurological rather than physical problems, the Veterans Administration probably felt reasonably certain that he no longer needed to receive disability compensation.

I don't know if he ever discovered that Barbara Knight's parents had written the letter tipping the VA off to his schemes. But, one thing was clear: my father's marriage to Barbara broke down within a few years for one reason or another. In February of 1953, they were divorced in Florida.

Barbara Adams Knight never remarried nor produced any heirs. She did not die of cancer and did not die young.

In reading the correspondence between my father and the VA, I found myself both perplexed and embarrassed. The ramblings of that man were foreign to me. My father always struck me as wise. Perhaps not a genius, but whomever was writing those letters had sounded like a complete idiot.

His medical evaluations also had numerous red flags. He continued to complain of a paranoia that "people do not believe I am an American." He repeated *ad nauseum* the desire to "put a Yankee pin on my back so they know I'm an American." He supported this by saying that people called him a "limey," a derogatory phrase for an Irishman, or accused him of being an Englishman. The doctor himself noted that my father "speaks in a peculiar way."

My father had no discernable accent.

Documentation from the VA revealed yet another in the seemingly endless Sonny Capone coincidences: toward the end of my father's service, before he was discharged, it was noted that he had a venereal disease marked by growths on his penis, and that he frequently ran high fevers. *Sonny Capone* (and I strain under the weight of my own repetition) is alleged to have contracted congenital syphilis from his father, Al. My father more than likely had congenital syphilis, too, explaining why I remember him as constantly feverish.

On a rare, recent occasion, I got up the nerve to ask my mother about this. Frankly, even now in my adulthood, it is still nerve-wracking for me to speak to my mother about almost anything, but particularly about my father.

"Did Dad have VD?"

It was a crass question, but I had no reason to sugarcoat any dialogues with my mother. She was taken aback at the abruptness and blunt nature of the question. She then pondered and replied pensively, "Maybe. He always wore a condom."

"And you never asked him why?"

And that was the end of any meaningful answers I would get from my mother on the subject.

In the end, the father I knew was not a concoctor of schemes and was not semi-literate. So why would he do those strange and abhorrent things after the war? Or was that him at all? Were there other motivations, other issues so deeply buried beneath the surface that simple conjecture could not explain them away?

I had to know. I had to learn more.

MARINER'S DOCUME

TES COAST GUARD

NAME	
William KNIGHT Jr.	

Z OR BK NUMBER	DATE OF BIR
████████████	7-14-25

PLACE OF BIRTH	CITIZEN
Illinois	USA

HOME ADDRESS

PO Box 2472
Tampa, Fla.

[signature]

SIGNATURE OF MARINE

Dad's Merchant Marine I.D.

In the Name of the Father, and of the Son, and of the Holy Ghost. Amen.

This Certifies that

William G. Knight

and

Genevieve M. De Ligny

were united by me in

Holy Matrimony

on *Sunday* the *second* day of *August* in the year of Our Lord One Thousand Nine Hundred and *Fifty Three*

at *First Congregational Church* in ~~the Diocese of~~ *Flushing* according to the form of Solemnization of Matrimony as contained in the Book of Common Prayer, and in accordance with the laws of the State of *New York* in the United States of America.

Dated *Sunday* the *second* day of *August* A.D. 19*53*.

Alfred Harry Rapp
Minister

WITNESSES:

Marie De Pietro.

Marriage Certificate

IX

THE MARRYING MAN

In February of 1953, my father was a single man again, but not for long. On August 2 of the very same year, he married a woman of French descent, named Genevieve DeLigny, in New York City—Flushing, Queens, to be exact.

My father was following a very strange and impulsive courtship pattern. None of the court documents from his divorce from Barbara Adams indicated marital infidelity. Yet less than six months later, he was at the altar again—and in another state, where he superficially appeared to have no family ties.

Now, New York City is still the Big Apple, and in the 1950s, it was considered the center of the known universe even more so than today. It would be paranoid of me to make too much of his draw to the locale. Yet still, the attraction to a place that had so many Capone ties cannot be completely dismissed. Were he to have settled in Atlanta, Pittsburg, Texas, Arizona or any number of almost infinite American destinations, it would be much tougher to connect the dots to Al Capone.

My father's paper trail still went boldly through the Veterans Administration system. In 1953, he was still checking in to VA healthcare facilities with numerous complaints—complaints unlike any I had heard during my attenuated lifetime with him: "Pain in the back of my head [his war wounds were in the *front* of his head]...dizzy at times...my right eye is not so good at times...I sleep poorly and I still continue to have blackouts."

He was also described by physicians as being immature and having a hostile attitude against society. Again, as I knew the man, nothing could be further from the truth. But, rather than simply going on what I, a man who had every reason to idealize his father, thought, I queried others. Talking with people who had known him during his younger days, people Mary Ann or I tracked down, not a single one could cite any of those characteristics. Discussions with folks who knew my father in his later years concurred that these were not the descriptions of the man they'd known as Bill Knight.

The medical evaluations droned on and on. Reading them was painful for me, as if it were a police blotter describing a rather unsavory and somewhat despicable man. I searched for that which was not redundant, which was no easy task. The 1953 documents mentioned his divorce from Barbara, noting that "*she* divorced *him*."

The marriage license for Bill Knight and Genevieve DeLigny was also the first documented appearance of the name that set me off on this entire quixotic journey. Listed as a witness to the wedding: Thor.

Thor, of course, was the boarding home owner in New York; geographically, it made sense that he appeared in my father's life when my father was in the Empire State. But, this took Thor's relationship with my father back to at least 1953, if not earlier.

Thor is now deceased and his daughter Jun Hae was unable to calculate exactly when he came into my father's life, or my father into his. But certainly, by the summer of 1953, they were close enough that he signed my father's wedding license.

Thor, Thor, Thor. The man drove me insane. Were he still alive, there was obviously so much he could tell me. And unlike so many others I would come across, he seemed willing to talk, at least within certain limits.

Jun Hae had said that Thor talked about my father all the time, and others said that Thor had Capone obsessions the way other people had Marilyn Monroe obsessions. Throughout this investigation, I often wondered if Thor's fan-obsessed delusions about Al Capone were just that—no different than a man who claimed Elvis was alive and working at a local gas station, and that they had long talks about hound dogs, blue suede shoes, and peanut butter and banana sandwiches.

But unlike such harmless fanaticisms, Thor's Capone hobby had created an obsession within my own life. He'd cast aspirations upon my own lineage, brought doubt upon the true identity of the man I'd known as my father. Far more dangerous stuff than an adoring fan or even a celebrity stalker. I never wished these questions or mysteries into my life. But Thor brought them there, and they weren't going away.

My father and Genevieve apparently lived for a time in New Jersey, not far from New York City, although my father indicated in correspondence that he planned on moving back to Florida sometime in the foreseeable future, although I have no record of that ever happening.

In trouble with the VA again, my father failed to report his changing marital status to them and thus, they chased him for disability monies paid to him as a married man, rather than the lesser amounts a single man would receive, during the short period while he was between quickie marriages. I could not help but chuckle as I read his official declaration of marital status in November, 1956: "2/2/48 to 2/53—Married to Barbara Adams. 8/2/53 Married to Genevieve DeLigny in New York. We are still married and as it looks we shall always be married." Sweet.

According to Jun Hae, my father never actually lived with Thor, but rather he stopped by from time to time, the way a traveling salesman might frequent the same small hotel or bed and breakfast. He and Thor became friends. Thor would later crop up in some of my father's adventures.

Perhaps Thor even introduced my father to Genevieve. I don't know. As much as I knew about my mother and as much as I uncovered about Barbara Adams, Genevieve was, for me, an enigma. Her marriage to my father lasted almost exactly the same amount of time as had his coupling with Barbara Adams: five years. Like Barbara, Genevieve appeared to have never remarried. She had no children with my father, nor did she appear to have any thereafter. She died only a few years ago.

Strange. Extraordinarily short courtships with two women, leading quickly to marriage. Each marriage lasting five years. No children. Both women never to marry again. Both women now deceased.

I started to wonder about my father and the issue he brought up in his most incoherent letter to the VA, the one where he said, "I went to a doctor and he run some test on me and found out that I am impotency unable to produce seaman [sic] in which make children…This is and may break up my home."

When my mother told me about my father wearing condoms, I assumed he was not chronically impotent. While my father was far from a genius, I would assume he knew the difference between impotence and sterility. Or did he? Furthermore, any schoolchild of a certain age knew that impotency did not mean that a person could not produce semen.

Untreated syphilis, whether congenital or otherwise, can cause sterility, although that is not one of the primary ways in which it presents. Sonny Capone, to make a point, had four children. My father had my sister and I, as well as the brother I never knew, who died before age one.

Why did my father not have children with his first two wives? I had no idea.

I always felt he *wanted* children, as he was such a loving, caring father to my sister and me. Childless couples in America in the 1940s and '50s were rare and usually only caused by sterility on the part of one partner or the other. Not that people *had* to have children, but it certainly was the baby-booming vogue.

So was my father sterile or frequently impotent? At that point, I did not know, nor may I ever. So, too, any certainty as to whether he lived most of his life with untreated congenital syphilis which, among other things, causes fevers as well as arthritic-like conditions. My father, when I knew him, was also arthritic. The clues and innuendos were all there, driving me slowly insane.

During the Genevieve years, my father continued his love affair with the sea. He worked both as a merchant seaman as well as a longshoreman. One day, as he was about to board a ship in the port of Bayonne, New Jersey, the ship exploded. Again. Luckily, this time, he was not already aboard and thus avoided critical injury.

Now, this was downright weird. It ranked right up there with getting struck twice by lightning. There were moments when I ruminated upon this and wondered if blowing up ships was a way that Al Capone's old enemies might have been gunning for his secret son, but that was far more drama than logic would support. If you want to kill someone, you don't go to all the trouble of blowing up gigantic ships. Too much trouble and too much collateral damage. But were I my father, I would have begun thinking twice about stepping aboard anything that floated.

It appeared that the seafaring days were what proved to be the death knell to my father's second marriage. Genevieve did not approve of his frequent absences, and so they divorced.

This, too, was strange. A woman who would give up her marriage due to her husband's inability to stay at home would most likely latch onto another man, a stay-at-home man, as soon as possible. But again, Genevieve did not remarry, living out the rest of her days a lonely, single woman. How odd.

Genevieve also, like Barbara before her, was alleged to have money. Was my father a gigolo? A fanciful thought. But, records did not back up the fantasy. Furthermore, how many gigolos claimed in writing to be impotent? On the other hand, it might have explained some other fiduciary issues that were to come up along the way in my father's life.

My father built a home for himself and Genevieve in Rahway, New Jersey. Yes, homes were far cheaper then; with the post-war building boom, the Levittowns of the sprawling, American suburbia were cropping up all over the place to service the returning US servicemen and their families. But there was a man still crying poverty to the VA while working as a laborer on or near ships. How did he afford to build a new home? Again, questions sprang up like dandelions in the spring, most without satisfactory answers.

And so in 1958, this 33-year-old (on paper) ex-Navy man, this longshoreman/merchant seaman, this traveler from Illinois to Idaho to the Philippines to Wisconsin to England to Florida to New York to New Jersey, became twice-married and now twice-divorced. This time, though, he did not rush into another short courtship and short marriage. This time, he waited three years, until 1961, to marry a 19-year-old woman named Elise Edeer. My mother.

Mom and Dad early 70's

X

MOM

America's fascination with the Mafia has popularized its lore and history. Apologists have tried reasoning that the psychology of Sicilians who ventured into this lifestyle followed an ingrained attitude of victimization and the need for survival. Mafia initiation involves pledging loyalty to a "house" or "family" that is meant to protect the weak against the abuse of the powerful.

Al Capone, of course, was the most famous American Mafioso, although his pure Mafia heritage might be brought into question, as he was not Sicilian, but rather Neapolitan. It is a fine point, as Naples, Capone's father's home, and Salerno, his mother's, are just north of Sicily, but still considered southern (versus northern) Italy.

Italy's attitude toward the north and the south is quite

similar to America's, with lingering rivalries, conflicts and distrusts lasting generations. Northern Italians often flinch at the embarrassment the Sicilians of the south have perpetrated upon them via their Mafia, whereas southern Italians bristle at such a generalized depiction of their heritage, much as southern Americans despise being characterized as hillbillies or Ku Kluxers.

My mother, Elise Edeer, is a first-generation American born to survivors of the Armenian genocide. I have often wondered, as my mother's occasional apologist, how this played into her own personal psychosis, her demons and her vitriolic attitudes toward personal survival.

The Armenian genocide is still a dirty little secret on the world stage, being forced more into the closet today due to its touchy ramifications against Muslims. Nearly one million Armenians were slaughtered in the years prior to and during World War I by the ruling class of the Ottoman Empire, the Muslims. The Armenians were of varying Christian faiths, both Catholic and Protestant derivations, with the Armenian Apostolic, better known today as the Armenian Orthodox Church, being the most popular insofar as having the largest number of Armenians as parishioners.

My mother married my father in a Greek Orthodox church, since the two denominations—Armenian Orthodox and Greek Orthodox—have similar customs based upon shared negative attitudes toward papal authority.

At the time of the Armenian genocide, my Grandma Dina—my mother's mother—was from a very prominent, well-to-do family in Turkey. As a little girl during the genocide, she had literally witnessed the mass killing of her entire family.

Only she and her sister had been saved. The rest of her family had been lined up outside their mansion and shot in the heads, gangland-style.

Observing this mass murder would have lingering effects on Grandma Dina's psyche, as might be expected. She eventually made her way over to America, to escape the horrific slaughter of innocent human beings in the name of religious zealotry. In Turkey, Armenians were regarded as infidels, to be treated as nothing more than animals, their rights to life and possessions rendered meaningless.

She eventually met my Grandpa Simon, who was also from Turkey. Simon, too, came from wealth and his grandfather, my great-great grandfather, had been a major general in the army. My mom has a picture and whenever I go home to visit her, she shows me that picture of my great-great grandfather, with all the medals on his uniform and his gleaming sword.

An uncle through marriage on my mom's side passed away in the late 1990s. He lived to almost 100; he'd been a taxidermist in New York City back in the day. With all the wealth her family had back in the old country, he would always refer to my mom as a princess, although her money was long since gone, long before she had even been born here in America.

I thought at times that he was talking solely about my mom's family, but now I think he might have also been talking about who my dad was. The rumored Capone money. Uncle Terry was his name. He was a wonderful old fellow.

I think Edeer was a shortening of their actual family name. My mother's relatives often spoke of a town named after my grandfather's family, although I have found no town of Edeer in modern day Turkey, nor any logical derivation thereof. Of course, with the extermination and expulsion of nearly all the Armenians, it is reasonable to assume that many towns' names were changed during the Muslim reign.

There is a unique attitude imprinted onto the soul of an ethnic, racial or religious survivor of sadistic execution or enslavement. African-Americans once held as slaves, and Jewish survivors of the Holocaust, can all attest to this lingering feeling, even as generations go by. It is justified paranoia, the need to always look over one's shoulder, to stash valuables away in odd places for safekeeping, and to have a heightened level of distrust toward those outside their cultural community. It is perhaps for these reasons that my mother's marriage to my father was an arranged one. Yes, an arranged marriage in the 1960s in America. How bizarre!

My mother's background, along with being born to genocide survivors, was an unusual one. Dina and Simon conceived her. Normal so far, right? But then, Grandma Dina had an affair with Simon's brother, Jack. This relationship produced another child, my Uncle Liam. Yes, they kept the baby and raised it as their own.

Well, not really. While Elise, my mother, was treated as well and was as loved as any child would expect to be, Liam was the literal "child locked in the attic." He was the embarrassment, the bastard child of an affair.

Liam and Elise had an obviously strained relationship that continues to this day. My father, though, got along quite well with Liam, as do I. While I was growing up, we—my family and I—visited with Liam quite frequently. But one can only imagine the tension that had to have existed between these two siblings. Elise and Liam were rivals, each striving for the affections of their mother, the rivalry punctuated by having two different fathers.

Simon and Jack, the two brothers and fathers, also led an odd existence, both working at the famed Waldorf-Astoria Hotel in Manhattan for many, many years. Imagine, two brothers, both in love with the same woman, both fathering children with her. Yet, one was married to her and the other wasn't.

Grandma Dina, in fact, had quite an emotional attachment to Jack, her brother-in-law. But Jack, too, was married, and was not about to leave his wife. And so all four people, related by blood, lust, occupation and marriage, continued along side-by-side until the end of their days. As with much else I came to discover about my family and extended family, how very, very strange and complicated this was. And clandestine.

And right in the middle of it all was the omnipresent Thor.

An arranged marriage for young, 19-year-old Elise. Why? Survivor mentality. One generation removed from the horrors of genocide, transplanted Armenians still lived lives of wariness and distrust—survival instincts were engrained within them and deservedly so. Elise needed to be "set up" and protected.

This can, and in this case *should* be looked at from every angle of what it means to be protected and taken care of. For a family attempting to marry off and safeguard young Elise, a strong man would make for a good choice of mate. A wise man, a man of the world, would also carry the preferred characteristics. A wealthy man would be the trifecta. And a kind, gentle man who would never put her in harm's way would be a grand slam.

William Knight, Jr. was cast in the role.

Huh?

With my father's ongoing physical maladies, so well documented via his correspondence with the VA, he would not appear to be the muscular, athletic he-man one would look to for physical protection. Older and wiser? That he was, being 14 years Elise's senior. Wealthy? That proved to be the strangest part of all. William Knight, a twice-divorced high school dropout and disabled Navy man constantly begging for greater government handouts, a worker on merchant ships, orphaned from birth, would not be anyone's idea of a wealthy man, nor was he. Or *was* he?

Ah, yes...Thor. He first turned up as a witness to my father's second marriage to Genevieve DeLigny in New York, where he owned a rooming house. Thor, it seems, was also friends with the brothers Edeer, my mother's father and uncle, who worked at the New York City Waldorf.

Thor, the aficionado of Al Capone lore, a man who once tried to buy one of Capone's homes, told Simon Edeer that his pal, Bill Knight, was Al Capone's son. Now, notoriety and infamy aside, this was big. Even those who'd only been in the States a short while had certainly heard of Al Capone, if they'd lived in America in the 1950s and early 1960s. *The Untouchables* television series, starring Robert Stack as Eliot Ness, premiered in October of 1959 and ran until September of 1963. It was produced by Desi Arnez and Desilu Studios, ironic in that Arnez had been a high school classmate of Sonny Capone. More ironic in that the Capone family sued Arnez (unsuccessfully) for using the likeness and name of their patriarch, Al, without permission or license. Ironic further to me personally, as Robert Stack would later star in a TV series called *Unsolved Mysteries.*

Unsolved mysteries. That was what my life had turned into.

But being linked by Thor to Big Al Capone, the *Capo di Tutti Capi*—the Boss of All Bosses—meant power, strength, protection and money, all of the things Elise's family desired for her. But how would Bill Knight, the one who lived hand to mouth throughout his entire life, pull off this charade, if it were indeed a charade?

I don't know.

Yet when Bill Knight appeared in Elise Edeer's life, he was living in the nice house he had built in Rahway, New Jersey (where was Genevieve? She didn't get the house in the divorce? How strange. Again, how very strange...), was driving a big convertible, and on their first date, he brought her to Coney Island and took her on all the rides. This was the image of an American success story, a great catch of a man in 1961. Handsome, well dressed, worldly and with a pocket full of cash, my father seemed to have come out of Central Casting. Elise, baby, this was marrying material!

An odd side note: one of the first things Elise did *not* like about my father was that he had a gay roommate in his house in Rahway. She brought that up to me only recently. How interesting. Was my father bisexual? Was it a totally platonic friendship, someone with whom to share the expenses who just *happened* to be gay? Nonetheless, Elise immediately thought ill of it and ordered my father to boot the man out, which Bill dutifully did. A forewarning of things to come in their soon-to-be stormy relationship? Perhaps.

And yet, both my mother and father portrayed theirs as an "arranged marriage." Arranged by my mother's parents and the inimitable Thor. The short courtship was merely a formality. From the time they first met to the day they got married, it was three months. It always intrigued me how fast they got married. I mean, from my father's perspective, it certainly beat his record of only 13 days before marrying Barbara Adams, wife number one.

So, after only a handful of dates, Bill Knight and Elise Edeer marched down the aisle, to the altar of the Holy Church of St. Nicholas, a Greek Orthodox church in Flushing, New York, the same city in which he had married Genevieve. On the marriage certificate, my mother indicated that this was her first marriage.

So did my father.

Well, obviously, this was a lie. Did my mother know he had been married twice before? I have no idea. She certainly *came* to know this, as did my sister and I growing up, although we were kept in the dark about the details.

Unlike the Roman Catholic Church, the Orthodox Church recognizes the reality of divorce, although it does not "grant" divorces. Divorced men and women are allowed to remarry under specific circumstances, such as infidelity, as judged by a spiritual court or bishop. It is regarded as a great tragedy, however, and a second marriage normally requires special permission from a bishop. A second wedding is always performed in the context of repentance on the part of the previously married party, a fact reflected in the ceremony.

Was my father merely trying to simplify things, to speed up the process by claiming to have never before been married, rather than waiting for special permissions? Possibly. The answer is quite plausible. But, there seems to be a string of lies tied to my father, lies and deceptions, none of which is in keeping with the character of the man who raised me. My father, my Bill Knight, would have just been honest and stoically gone through the ecumenical process, knowing that it was simply that: a process, and one that would eventually turn his way.

My mother was a virgin on her wedding night. The happy couple, still relative strangers to each other, honeymooned in Fort Lauderdale, Florida, quite the vacation spot in January of 1961. There, it seemed that everywhere they went, everyone knew Bill Knight. But, not Bill Knight, the orphaned, high school dropout, Midwestern farmhand or poor merchant seaman. No, this Bill Knight was quite the social butterfly. A real playboy, the life of the party. My mother asked him how this all came about. My father explained that he had owned a popular restaurant there in Florida, where everyone who was anyone seemed to know good old Bill.

Huh? I say again…huh?

This was the first and last time I would hear anything about my father, the "restaurateur." I checked all sorts of public records and did all types of fact checking. Bill the restaurateur seems to be an imaginary figment of a man creating a grandiose past completely devoid of fact or truth.

Yet why the attention from strangers? Wintering north-erners and native Floridians, all giving a big "hi-hello" and a slap on the back to their pal, Bill?

I cannot for the life of me figure it out.

But what set me off on this search was the tip-off from Thor. The Al Capone tale. My father as the son of Big Al Capone. Florida was where Capone ended his career. The Capone family pretty much settled and stayed there for the most part during the '50s and early '60s. My father had married a Floridian—his first wife, Barbara. At one point, he claimed to me that he had lived for a time during his childhood, prior to his life on the Buzick farm, at a Florida mansion. Now, there he was in Florida again, honeymooning, and certainly showing off for his new third wife, the child bride Elise.

Fort Lauderdale was, like most major American cities in the 1960s, a Mafia hotbed. But, there was a unique linkage there, the remaining Capones' residence in Florida notwith-standing. By the '60s, almost all crooked roads led back to New York City and the famed Five Families: the Bonannos, the Colombos, the Genoveses, the Gambinos and the Luccheses. These five powerhouses had their fingers in every major organized crime operation in America, regardless of location. Their only true competition: the remnants of Al Capone's old Chicago gang, now led by Tony "Big Tuna" Accardo and his right-hand man and primary Fort Lauderdale mechanic, Sam "Momo" Giancana.

In the '60s Giancana would gain fame as the Mafioso alleged to have been recruited by the CIA to bump off Fidel Castro, an operation to be launched out of, yes, Florida. Giancana was also the man who shared the same lover as

President Kennedy—Judith Campbell—and was singer Frank Sinatra's closest mob connection.

Giancana's personal Florida right-hand man was Santo Trafficante, Jr. In 1963, Trafficante and New Orleans mob boss Carlos Marcello were the wise guys alleged to have conspired to assassinate JFK, if one were to believe the Mafia connection to that particular conspiracy theory. My father would also go on to tell me of time spent in New Orleans. Doing what exactly? Helping plan JFK's assassination? I jest...

My father's continued propensity to wind up right where Capone's gang had their talons never ceases to amaze me. Was it by design? Was he occasionally summoned? Did he seek them out for a hand out from time to time? Or was he, like Thor, some obsessed fan? I have no idea. But putting aside the fact that Florida in the early 1960s was a popular honeymooning and vacationing spot, my mother and I both find it intriguing that my father seemed like such a celebrity down there.

My mom didn't know how to swim; therefore, she almost drowned in the hotel pool in Florida during their honeymoon. She told me how my dad didn't even flinch to save her. My mom almost felt that he was going to let her drown in the pool, but at the last minute, one of his buddies dove in and saved her. She was like, "That bastard wouldn't even jump in to save me!"

I have to admit, I chuckled a bit at the retelling of this story. This whole journey has been rife with drama, intrigue and heart-break for me. Yet even this anecdote raises serious questions. No, I do not think my father was hoping to watch his new bride drown on their honeymoon. There was no upside to that, although I'm sure there were times during their marriage when he wished he had it all to do over again, that he could maybe trip his friend as he was about to play lifeguard with her.

But, my father had been a Navy man. They don't put you on ships if you can't swim. Think about it. Maybe the whole thing was a figment of my mother's imagination, a representation of the anger she felt throughout her life at being "married off," not allowed to find her own true love, but forced into a life someone else chose for her. I don't know. But my father certainly *could* swim and I doubt he'd have been so neglectful as to let her die on him at that point in their relationship.

As a wedding present, my father gave my mother the keys to a brand new Buick convertible. Not just the keys, but the whole car, too. Whenever I was a kid and we would go over the George Washington Bridge, my mom would reminisce about that new convertible. She talked about how my dad drove her over that very bridge into New Jersey, her hair waving in the wind, and how much she enjoyed the trip. I always think about that when I go over the GWB, to go home to visit my mom, and I start to get teary-eyed thinking about what it was like. Good times. Some rare, good times.

My father then went out and bought a chain of dry cleaning stores. Not just one store, but a whole string of them up in northern New Jersey. Happy with her financial windfall as she was, my mother asked, "Bill, where are you getting the money?"

"Oh, don't worry about it, Granny."

Their pet names for each other were "Old Man" and "Granny." "Old Man" seemed a natural considering their age difference. "Granny" was most likely my father's attempt at humorously parrying her thrust.

Well, Granny may not have worried about it, but I am perplexed by it. Building a house in post-war America was one thing; buying new convertibles and opening up chains of stores as easily as buying French fries at a McDonald's was quite another. There was nothing—no paper trail, no records of any sort—that would substantiate how or where my father came into enough money to live that level of lifestyle. None. No credible explanation. And where credible explanation departs, wilder theories are all that is left.

Capone money?

That's what my mother suspected. That's what her father suspected. That's what her brother Liam suspected. That's what Thor professed. None would go on record with me as stating that the words came directly from my father's own lips, but all of them took it as gospel, like the earth being round and the sun setting in the west. Bill Knight was Al Capone's son and Capone money made Bill financially flush—not living the life of a millionaire, but certainly living the American dream, relatively comfortable and able to take on a "what, me worry?" attitude regarding how to pay the next set of bills that lay waiting for him in the mailbox.

My father, Al Capone's son. Swinging in Florida with his teenage bride, setting up shop just outside the Big Apple in New Jersey, and able to provide protection, financially and otherwise, to the daughter of a scared, Armenian refugee family. Life for Bill and Elise Knight was good. Life, as I see it today, looking upon it 40-odd years later, was very, very confusing and mysterious.

Buzick Farm 2006

XI

BACK TO THE FARM

Lillian Myrtle King Nesson Buzick Craig Lott Wedeking. Quite a mouthful. Right up there with Elizabeth Taylor Hilton Wilding Todd Fisher Burton Burton Warner Fortensky. Only the second lady is a famous Academy Award-winning actress and icon, and the other is…a mystery.

Previously referred to here as Mrs. Buzick, Lillian Buzick, with her husband James, took in a boy referred to as William Knight, Jr., and for a time raised him as their own.

And perhaps he was. I mean *really* was.

My mother uncovered something peculiar when she married and moved in with my father. Those VA checks, those infamous VA checks he had so fought for after his military service in the '40s and '50s, were not enriching him at all.

Whatever was left after he sent some of those meager dollars off to his previous two wives (although my mother could find no divorce decrees mandating him to do so) was mailed off to...Lillian Buzick. For all of his arguing and scamming, it would appear that my father never actually kept a dime of that VA money for himself.

Why, why, why, why?

I have no idea. And again, where a situation is devoid of a logical answer...wilder conjectures are free to roam the landscape.

My mother immediately put a halt to this madness, which was particularly mad, in her opinion, because many of the checks to Lillian were coming back, indicating that the recipient had moved. My father apparently fought my mother on this and continued trying to get these checks into Lillian's hands well into the mid-1960s, when finally, it was indicated that Lillian had, in fact, died. The checks to the ex-wives were less a point of contention; my father willfully complied with my mother's requests.

Now remember, it was James Buzick whom my father loved and adored. It was James Buzick whose untimely death brought my father out of the Navy during wartime, so that he could save the family farm in Illinois. Lillian was the woman who, to assuage her depressed widowhood, went scampering off with a young soldier not much older than my father at the time, embarrassing my dad and causing him to leave the farm for good. He had been disgusted with Lillian's behavior and felt that the farm was going nowhere so long as Lillian ignored his advice on how to run it properly and profitably.

If my father had so clashed with this woman and cut off ties with her, why did he continue to financially support her? Lillian went on to marry four more times. Surely, one or more of those men could keep a roof over her head. I mean, it wasn't as if my father's VA money was very much to begin with. He was deemed only 30 percent incapacitated, not totally disabled. The money was a pittance.

My father was a soft touch. Every charity in town knew they could count on Bill Knight to help them out. Judging by the turnout at his funeral, I am sure that he helped out many down-on-their luck individuals as well. He was that kind of man, at least during the years I had known him. And yes, over the ensuing years, my mother felt the need to put her foot down when that charitable largesse went beyond what she felt was right and in his own family's best interest.

So who was Lillian, exactly?

In a 1930 census, James C. Buzick was listed with a house-keeper, Myrtle K. Nesson. Not Lillian, her first name, but Myrtle, her middle name. Odd…It would appear that King was her maiden name and that Nesson was from a first marriage.

Or not. I tracked down a sister-in-law of Lillian/Myrtle who claimed she was married a total of four times, so if one were to believe that, pick any two names and throw them out of the mix, or else chalk it up to poor memory. Heck, I'm sure some of Elizabeth Taylor's most ardent fans have just as hard a time keeping *her* marriages straight.

By 1941, when my father allegedly came on the scene at the Buzick farm, James and Lillian/Myrtle were husband and wife. Over time, Lillian appears to have used the name Myrtle, switching back and forth with no real logic or reason. Her death certificate listed Myrtle as her first name, Lillian as her middle name, flip-flopping it from how it appeared elsewhere. And as I've come to believe, where reason is absent...

In the address book my father left me when he died (or should I say, the one I purloined from my mother, who was throwing all of his things out), she was listed as Myrtle. Her last known address was in Metropolis, Illinois. Her obituary listed her as having died in 1964. It mentioned no children. Her sister-in-law told me she died destitute, living in a trailer park.

I took this issue to the indomitable Mary Ann, my wise lead-tracker. She in turn farmed some of the work out to various genealogists in her network, searching for the whys and where-fores of the former Mrs. Buzick. What came back was intriguing.

For one thing, Myrtle—or Lillian, as you may—was almost exactly the same age as...Irene Maude Meis. Yes, the woman listed on my father's birth certificate as his mother. The 19-year-old woman with no traceable birth, death or life in between.

Myrtle Lillian King was born in Danville, Kentucky, on March 18, 1905. Irene Maude Meis allegedly gave birth to William Knight, Jr., on July 14, 1925, when she was 19 years old. Myrtle Lillian King would have been approximately 20 years, four months old. Furthermore, while there exist no records of an Irene Maude Meis or any logical derivation of that name having been born in Danville, Illinois, as she listed on my father's birth certificate, how strange that Myrtle Lillian

King was also born in Danville—only in this case, Danville, Kentucky.

There are 15 states with Danvilles in the United States. Thus, it is a fairly common town name, but what are the chances that both my father's foster mother and his real mother would be from towns in different states with that same name? There are 18,218 towns or cities in the United States. The U. S. population in 1905 was almost 84 million. The two women were allegedly born within months of one another. The chances of this coincidence are infinitesimal.

My Mary Ann even physically visited Danville, Illinois, for me. There is absolutely, positively no record of any woman who could have possibly been Irene Maude Meis having lived or been born there under that name at the time that she claimed. In further investigation, Mary Ann turned up no Irenes or Maudes in Myrtle's immediate family—no sister or female cousin she might have been covering for. None of Myrtle's female siblings were of similar age, nor were any old enough to have been a potential grandparent to my father.

Myrtle's family moved from Kentucky to Illinois by 1907. Myrtle's mother liked weddings as well, having been wed four times herself. Jeez! I have a father married three times, his foster mother was married between four and six times, and *her* mother married four times. Do some research and you turn up the craziest things! My ancestors kept the entire rice industry solvent.

The Kings settled in Bloomington, Illinois, about 130 miles southwest of Chicago. Were Myrtle to have found herself in the family way, traveling to Chicago to have the baby and put it up for adoption is not out of the realm of possibility.

Melvin, Illinois, where the Buzick farm was located, was only about 50 miles east of Bloomington and about 100 miles due south of Chicago. Quite the interesting triangulation.

Al Capone, for what it's worth, moved from New York City to Chicago (Cicero, Illinois) in 1919. This relates to the overall picture by means of mentioning again that my father was supposedly born in 1925, making it plausible that Capone was his father. Sonny Capone was born in 1919 in New York, *just prior* to Big Al's moving to Illinois. Ralphie Capone, Ralph "Bottles" Capone's son, was born in 1917 in New York.

This plays into the questions of whether Al Capone was my father's father, and whether Myrtle King was his mother. If so, a 1925 birth date, such as was represented on his birth certificate, in Chicago, makes the most sense. I raise this because, obviously, my father required not only a father, but a mother as well; that's usually how these things work.

Myrtle was within a reasonable drive of Chicago most of her life, with the exception of her first few years on earth. Mary Ann was never able to place Myrtle *in* Chicago, via census records or the like, but one cannot rule out her visiting the City Of Big Shoulders or, perhaps, living there a short while— say, a few months or so.

Bloomington, Illinois, where Myrtle was raised, was on nostalgic old Route 66. It connected directly via that famed route to...Al Capone's Chicago. Capone, in fact, was a primary behind-the-scenes supporter of getting Route 66 paved, believing correctly that a paved highway would make bootleg-ging getaways much faster for his criminal enterprise. Funny how Capone was able to lobby for so many populist notions while in doing so, he set himself up as a more successful criminal. Route 66 wound its way from Chicago to St. Louis and then on to sunny California. Al Capone and his gang used it extensively.

So, were there other ways in which Mr. Capone was getting his kicks on Route 66? Bedding down some young Bloomington girl, perhaps? It's possible. It's even probable. Capone did not treat Chicago as an island prison from which he would never escape. His criminal activities stretched hundreds of miles in each direction. There were people out there in the boondocks, and people were customers. Furthermore, Al needed places for bootlegging supplies as well as hiding places for men, materials and moolah.

Theory: it is possible and plausible that my father's true blood parents were Myrtle Lillian King and Alphonse Capone. Perhaps my father *was* born in 1925 or thereabouts. Perhaps it was in Chicago, perhaps not. It may have been anywhere in Illinois. His only birth certificate was a fake; that I've come to realize. The document contained a registration number that fit in consecutively with others around it, meaning that the other birth certificates immediately before and after it were for births around the same time period. So, it is doubtful that even if it were a fake, it would not have been filed a long time before or after July 14, 1925.

My father could have been born sometime before that date and the paperwork not submitted until then. He could have been born, for example, in 1923, and Myrtle may have waited until the summer of 1925 to tell Capone of the incident. It is said that Capone forced his mistresses to have abortions, whether they cared to or not. Maybe Myrtle waited until the baby was born to spring it all on him.

Capone may have been a monster in many ways, but killing live babies seems a bit low even for him. So, perhaps Myrtle went to him for assistance, he arranged a birth certificate in Cook County, Chicago, where he practically ran the joint, and had a birth certificate drawn up, giving the child a name and manufacturing the names of parents. Myrtle, single and poor, allowed the child to go into the foster care system. Capone kept an eye out—it was his child, his blood.

A few years later, Myrtle had herself a man, a good man: James Buzick. As the child had been tracked carefully through the foster care system, he was easily located and dumped on the doorstep of the Buzick farm in Melvin, Illinois. Did James Buzick know who the kid's real parents were? Maybe, maybe not. The theory does not depend upon it one way or the other. Nonetheless, Bill Knight (Knight... A knight works for a king. Myrtle King! Meis was a famous name of a chain of department stores in Cook County. It all fits!) finally had a nuclear family.

Along the way, we have shortterm reminisces of time spent in a mansion in Florida. Perhaps for a short time, my father was between foster care homes, and Al took him in. Passed him off as a son of a friend or something of that sort. Who knows?

Then, Jim Buzick died while my father was in the Navy. Bill returned to the farm, but conflicted with Myrtle, who unbeknownst to him, was his birth mother. Myrtle acted in a rather un-window-like way, but then again, this was a woman who did her share of running around and marrying around, so no big surprise there. Still, my father sent her money throughout the '40s and '50s. Guilt? Feelings of responsibility? All quite logical. Then, she died.

The road could end there, I know it. But then again, I don't know it. Proving a theory like this is almost impossible. Myrtle listed no other children. Mary Ann and I located no other close blood relatives. Thus, tracking down someone for a DNA test appears difficult to almost impossible at this juncture. And yet, there is the flip side of the coin: the theory can also not be *disproved*.

To add to it all, on some other documents I found in the treasure trove of the VA, another name was mentioned: Julia Ferne Sherman—grandmother of William Knight, Jr. An alternate next-of-kin for my father. And, Julia Ferne Sherman (a.k.a. Fern Sherman) matches...nothing. Did she exist? Yes. Mary Ann tracked her records down, too. Was she related to Myrtle? No. Al Capone? No. Jim Buzick? No. William Knight, Sr.? No. Irene Maude Meis? No. Elizabeth Taylor? No. She simply pops up amidst it all, as incongruous as a tree growing in the middle of the ocean. A name picked out of a telephone book. Perhaps, at best, the mother or grandmother of a childhood friend. Fern Sherman's family seemed all plainly accounted for. No clues leading one to believe there was a bastard child in her life, or family, who was born between 1917 and 1925 and later discreetly shuffled away somewhere.

Fern Sherman. The truth to who I am, the crux of this journey of mine, could be summed up in a *non sequitur* as obtuse and disconnected as that name. Fern Sherman. I'm chasing shadows, searching for truth, and everywhere I turn, there's Al Capone. But whenever I reach out to grab him, a Fern Sherman stands in my way.

Buzick Farm 2006

Funeral Services Held Tuesday for Myrtle Wedeking

Mrs. Myrtle L. Wedeking, 59, of 801 East 6th Street, died October 4 at the Massac Memorial Hospital.

Funeral services were held Tuesday at the Miller Funeral Home Chapel, with the Rev. O. L. Angel officiating. Interment was in the Masonic cemetery. Pallbearers were as follows: William A. Wedeking, B. R. Wedeking, Coy Wedeking, Noah Windhorst, Ruben Windhorst and Tom Anderson.

Mrs. Guy Cagle and Mrs. Charles Fitch were the singers and the organist was Mrs. Leroy Barger.

The following obituary was read at the service:

Myrtle Lillian Wedeking passed away Sunday morning at the Massac Memorial Hospital. She was born March 18, 1905 in Danville, Kentucky, and had reached the age of 59 years, 6 months and 16 days.

She was a member of the First Christian Church of Metropolis.

In July, 1961, she was united in marriage to Elmer Wedeking.

She leaves to mourn her passing, her husband, Elmer; two sisters, Mrs. Bessie Busick of California, and Mrs. Martha Bough of Bloomington; two brothers, John and Robert King, both of Bloomington; several nieces, nephews, other relatives and friends

JAMES CLIVE BUZICK

James Clive Buzick, son of Nelson and Sarah Mariah (Woolsoncroft) Buzick was born on a farm just west of Roberts, Illinois, August 14th, and died in Roberts, Tuesday, March 16th, 1943, aged 52 years, 7 months and 2 days.

In September 1905, the family moved to Champaign, Illinois, where James graduated from high school and attended the University of Illinois. While at the university he was affiliated with the Chi Psi fraternity.

During World War No. 1, he enlisted in the U. S. Army and served in the 870th Aero Squadron. Within a few months after the signing of the Armistice he returned to Roberts to manage his father's farm. A few years later he left the farm to care for his invalid father. After the death of his father in 1925, he returned to the farm. This time, however, to the farm southwest of Roberts.

January 12, 1931, he married Lillian Myrtle King who survives him. He also leaves one brother and three sisters. These are John Buzick, of Monette, Arkansas, Mrs. F. C. Ringeisen of Toledo, Ohio, Mrs. Stanley Leak of Kankakee, Illinois and Mrs. O. L. Grismore, of Washington, D. C.

Mr. Buzick was an active member of the community taking an active part in public affairs. He was a member of the American Legion Post No. 642 at Melvin where he served as commander during 1939. He filled other offices at various times and was always prompt in performing the duties thus assigned him.

Funeral services were held in the Methodist Church in Roberts, Saturday, March 20th at two o'clock P. M., Rev. John T. Killip and Rev. P. Bear officiating. Burial was in Lyman cemetery. The services at the grave were by the American Legion.

RETURNS FROM HOSPITAL

Mrs. John Iler was able to return to her home here last week following a serious operation at the Research Hospital in Chicago some time ago. She is recovering nicely and spent several days with her sister-in-law, Mrs. Frank Shear in Thawville.

Obituary for Myrtle Wedeking and James Buzick

St Gaudin Gold Coin

XII

THE FAMILY JEWELS

In tracing my family's history, I have managed to amble clumsily in the dark to this point in time, the relative present. My father, William Knight, Jr., and my mother, Elise Edeer Knight, were married and went on to have my older brother—who died while still a baby—myself, and my younger sister. All was good…Well, "all was all" would be more to the point.

Prior to my birth, back in the 1960s, my father opened a chain of dry cleaning stores in North Jersey. There was no logical reason why any bank would loan him that kind of money. He appeared to have no collateral. Yes, he owned a house, but there was no reasonable explanation as to where he would have gotten the down payment for that.

If one were to speculate that Bill Knight was a good saver, tight with a buck, he may have scraped together a down payment, but he would had to have mortgaged all the rest, thus making his house in Rahway worthless as business collateral. My father had no real parents—thus, no inheritance. His jobs were blue collar, working class. Despite this, the house in Rahway was rather nice

But the Bill-the-Saver guise was belied by his penchant for new-model convertibles, among other delectables. Which brings me back to what no one who knew my father could ever claim to have heard him say with his own lips: that he was Al Capone's son, and that his riches in life were tied somehow to the Big Boss of Chicago.

But Capone died in 1947. The story has moved to the 1960s. How was Bill Knight getting Capone money then?

Theories abound. One ties in well with the total information blockades I have run into while trying to discover my father's true roots.

Al Capone's estate is not to be measured only in dollars and cents, but in influence and organization. This is the Mafia, after all. The phrases "gang influence" and "Mafia influence" proliferate in our modern culture. Politicians who are said to be "mobbed up" may not necessarily be on mob payrolls, but are being protected or blackmailed, perhaps, by underworld organizations in return for favors only they can deliver.

Back scratchers scratch other people's backs. Likewise, only stoolies talk. Al Capone may be dead, but the remnants of his legacy remain—the Chicago mob and its tributaries. Some things you just don't talk about. At least, that's what I've run into when I've tried to get people to talk to me.

Perhaps my father had been given some seed money at

some point in order to establish a decent life for himself. That would be a magnanimous thing for Alphonse Capone to do for his illegitimate child. But when and how could he have given that to him? Again, bear in mind the timeline. As of 1947—no more Al Capone. My father showed little in the way of wealth until well into the late 1950s.

Ralph Capone remains a possibility. He lived until 1974 and was basically the remaining Capone family tie to the old days of the Chicago mob. Yet, his later years were scarred with intimidation and harassment from a federal government still feeling the sting of embarrassment from the lavish and pugnacious lifestyle and fame of his brother Al. Ralph ended his life residing in a modest apartment, above a garage outside of Mercer, Wisconsin. In 1961, while still being hounded on tax evasion issues, he testified to having only $20,000 in cash to his name, and nothing more.

Now, it's easy to surmise that this was all a clever ruse. Shortly before his move to the attic apartment, Ralph owned Raycap Lodge on Big Martha Lake in Northern Wisconsin. Raycap (named for Rayola and Capone—his parents' last names) had been a regional hot spot for lavish parties for moneyed swells. Most Mafioso knew to live small, not large, with brother Al the poster child for what happened when a crime boss drew too much attention to himself. Perhaps Ralph was wise enough to squirrel away enough filthy lucre to keep himself well through the end of his days. Obviously, the federal government hypothesized the same, or why else would they continue stalking him in search of such riches?

Could Ralph, childless since his namesake son committed suicide in 1950, have spotted Bill Knight some cash as a goodwill gesture? The theory has validity.

An issue from early in my parents' marriage was that when my mother met my father, he was a traveling man, and for her, that would not do. It was only then that the dry cleaning store concept came to fruition. A kind of job where Bill would remain close to home.

But in the late '60s, the cities of North Jersey became hotbeds of racial tension and unrest. Newark, Paterson, Jersey City and Elizabeth all had massive violence and upheaval. Many of my father's stores were burned out in the carnage. It was time to move into a new line of work.

My father became an independent trucker. He bought a rig and almost immediately began hauling for Union Carbide.

Now, buying your own semi rig was not cheap. Much like starting your own string of dry cleaners. And unlike opening a dry cleaners, becoming a successful, independent trucker required connections. After all, you didn't make money driving that thing around empty. How did quiet Bill Knight manage to buy that rig and tool on over to big, multinational Union Carbide and immediately land himself a regular route? It gives the mind pause.

I can still recall going over to Union Carbide with my dad, having him introduce me to executives and watching them treat my father, the trucker, like an equal. Something now seems wrong with that picture. Were strings pulled? Did someone owe someone a favor? Was my father "connected" in some way?

My father's truck driving days were the times of my youth, and my fondest and most vivid memories of him. Whereas I wonder today how he afforded to set himself up in business, that truck was a traveling disaster. Old, filled to the brim with junk, no air conditioning, no heat, an old radio as the only companionship when he went on runs, it was incredibly uncomfortable, even for a truck. My dad would also never be without his trusty jar of jellybeans, his favorite snack and mine. Well, "jar" is being diplomatic. More like a gigantic jug filled with those multicolored morsels of fruity, sweet taste.

There was nothing and everything to love about being in that truck with my dad. It was a pleasure I usually only got to experience on the weekends, as he claimed to be driving cross-country during most of the week, every week. He suffered greatly from arthritis and downed nearly a bottle of anti-inflammatories every day. He was also reckless as all get out. I can so richly recall seeing him on his back underneath the cab, tinkering with something or another, oil and gasoline all around and on him, while a lit cigarette dangled precariously from his lower lip. What, me worry?

He was also an independent, meaning he was not a union member. This was a dangerous thing. The teamsters often went on strike. Meanwhile, my father, an independent, kept on driving. Scab drivers were often threatened and even shot at by strikers. Still, Bill kept on driving.

My father never carried credit cards. His pockets were always bulging with rolls of hundred dollar bills. In the '60s and '70s, he regularly made two to three thousand dollars per week. For a blue collar guy, I would imagine this to be a lot of money for that time.

When my father was away, my mother would hoard. My father left bankbooks lying all over the house—dozens upon dozens of them, all showing significant amounts of money in the accounts. It seemed that whenever my father was out of town, my mother would go through those books, get in her car, and drive on over to whichever bank had some money, forge his name, and drain the account.

My father, being no dummy, would discover this soon after returning home, and fighting would ensue. Vicious, terrible fighting. And what did my mother do with the money? Nothing. Absolutely nothing. No shopping sprees, no new clothes or cars. She'd just steal Bill's money and squirrel it away for herself. No rhyme or reason. Survivor mentality. Sequester valuables in case the Turks come to burn down your village.

The million dollar question: where did all this money come from? How did my father get so connected so quickly and so easily? Wait, that's two questions. Oh, hell, the questions are neverending.

Perhaps the biggest money question came after my father died. My mother, while liquidating the last of the bank accounts she hadn't already robbed, found records of a safe deposit box. Frankly, she found lots of safe deposit boxes. But one was of particular interest.

She dragged me and my sister along as she strolled into the bank. Being out in public with my mother was always gut wrenching. Her ability to make a scene over nothing as simply a matter of course gave me a nervous stomach. As we gingerly walked into the vault, the bank manager left and my mother commenced to open the large box. As she peeled back the lid, the three of us stared at a mountain of gold coins—hundreds and hundreds of them.

"Get out! Get out!" she screeched at me and my sister. Scared, we dutifully exited the vault, leaving her alone with her fortune. *Our* fortune.

How did he get it? Dozens and dozens of bank accounts full of money. Rolls of hundreds; thousands and thousands of dollars of liquidity, always on hand. Safe deposit boxes, at least one overflowing with valuable gold coins. A house. A big, semi tractor-trailer. New convertibles nearly every year. None of it made any sense. It didn't make sense then and it doesn't make sense now. Bill Knight's wealth was unexplainable. Unless…

Theories for unexplained wealth are infinite, especially when mob connections are brought into the equation. But this whole Capone thing only came to my attention after my father passed away. Prior to that, all I had to go on, if there were any questions in my mind at all, were what I saw and heard around me.

There were certain oddities, I remember, while growing up. The talk of living for a time in a Florida mansion—that still throws me. His tales of it were so vivid. A fishpond in the front yard. He loved to look at the colorful, tropical fish. A Rolls Royce. He even once told me he owned his own Rolls, shortly before he married my mother.

Were these just fanciful tales a father would tell a son? Did he tell tales like these for my mother, for Thor, for others he met? If so, why did they believe him? Was everyone he met so gullible? What would lead any of them to believe such talk?

Money.

Drive up in a new convertible, reach into your pocket for a roll of hundreds, and have a safe deposit box full of gold, and yes, people would easily believe you were the illegitimate son of the most famous gangster of all time.

Perhaps he was indeed staked a small fortune by Ralph Capone or some other family contact, as part of Al's final wishes in the settlement of his estate. Or perhaps there is another simple step of logic to be taken. My father spent years traveling in the late '50s. He would later travel extensively again, once he started his trucking business in the late '60s and beyond. My father would sometimes go for weeks at time, traveling a lot through the Midwest, by his own accounts. Kentucky comes to mind, in particular, as well as Illinois. States where Capone and Chicago mob influence had a strong foothold.

Maybe my father *was* connected, and not just by blood. Who knows what he was carrying in that truck? Lord knows I don't. Perhaps Bill Knight wasn't simply given a handout, but a business opportunity. After all, such was the family business.

I asked my mother the other day about the coins. She said she still has them, that they rightfully belong to my sister and me, and that we'll get them when our time comes—when she, too, passes away. As many issues as I have with the woman, this much is true: the survivor mentality remains. She has not gone through all of Bill's money. Not yet, anyway. And I doubt she ever will. One, there seems to be a never ending supply of it and two, the Turks may still be coming.

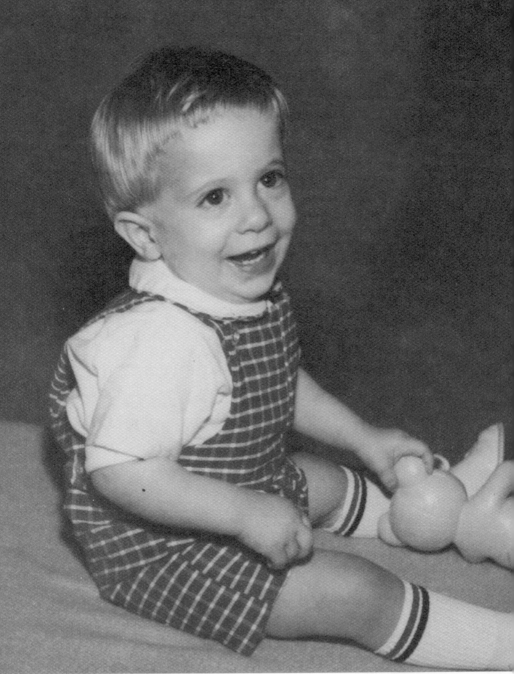

Me at 1 year old

XIII

WHO'S YOUR DADDY?

"I went to a doctor and he run some test on me and found out that I am impotency unable to produce seaman [sic] in which make children... This is and may break up my home."

Information I've been able to gather from the Veterans Administration has been a blessing and a curse. It's provided me with some astonishingly unabashed conundrums, such as the paragraph above, as well as a plethora of pages detailing every damn flu shot my father ever received while in the service, or while qualified to receive veterans' benefits. In total, I have about two full reams of paper courtesy of our government, and I've become bleary-eyed trying to make my way through it all.

Along the way, I've spoken at length to relatives and friends, as well as people I've come to know as friends or acquaintances of my father. Many have slammed doors in my face or phones in my ear. That weirds me out, making me so suspicious that my father was indeed a man of mystery, most likely some form of relative or connection to Al Capone or his family. Others have been far kinder, but still frustrating in their inability or unwillingness to give me exactly the type of information I need in order to draw any substantial conclusions, either proving or disproving this theory.

Uncle Liam comes to mind. I love my mother's half-brother. He's always been kind to me. I've discussed my father numerous times with him and he's confirmed that he has always taken at face value that my father was indeed Al Capone's son. The frustrating part is that he's offered me nothing in the way of proof. Perhaps he has none.

This search is like asking people the meaning of life. Those of faith simply say they believe in God or in a god. That's why they call it faith. In this case, I've been trying to find more.

So Uncle Liam, under the duress of my incessant questioning, drops this little bomb on me: "There's a clue in the VA medical records."

"What?"

"You'll see."

See what I mean? Even people who claim to want to help me turn it into a parlor game.

So I hunch over these piles of papers, something as banal as a well visit taking up three pages or more. After all, this is the government. And then I find it: a request for a psychiatric opinion as to whether my father was fit to be an adoptive parent.

Thunk!

As if things could get much worse. Here I am, spending countless hours and money trying to find out the true identity of William Knight, Jr., and now I'm thrown by the fact that William Knight, Jr. may not even be my real father. Thanks a lot, Uncle Liam.

Of course, I pounced on this like a stalking cat. "Am I adopted?" I asked Liam, and my mother. I was willing to ask anyone I could in order to find if anyone would crack, if they'd split off from the same script the others might have been reading from.

Uncle Liam crumbled first. "I don't *think* you're adopted. But…"

"But what?"

"You should talk to your mother."

"But you were the one who told me I'd find a clue in the VA records. I've looked through everything over and over. I find nothing that directly and definitively links my father to Al Capone, but now I find this thing that says my father applied to be an adoptive parent."

"Well, I just know there's a possibility that you might not be your father's son."

This is the sort of thing that hits a person like a ton of bricks. I began staring at every picture I had of myself and of my father. When I was much younger, I favored him. Later in life, today, I do not. Oddly enough, I resemble pictures I've seen of Sonny Capone. Just as oddly, I resemble Al Capone. I resemble Capone far more than my father resembled him. How does someone explain this to me?

I have a sister whom I am quite close to. I shared this with her. In my anxiety, I forgot that this affects her the same way it affects me. "Then who am I, Chris? *Are* we related?"

I had to call Uncle Liam again. "Look, there's something fishy here. Either my mother—your sister—had babies or she didn't. This can't be that complicated."

Uncle Liam hemmed and hawed. "Your mother had babies. But I think there was a problem. That's why your mother and father talked about adopting. As I recall, your father may have been sterile."

Well, at least Uncle Liam knew the difference between sterility and impotence. "So if my mother had babies, then who am I?"

"Her son. I think she went to a doctor for artificial insemination."

I'd heard of artificial insemination, but I knew little about it. As with many other things in this journey, I eventually became drawn into learning an enormous amount about something I had never dreamed I'd be researching. But before that, it was back to my mother, something I loathed doing.

"Am I adopted?"

"No."

"Then why did you and Dad look into adoption?"

"I hate talking about your father. Let it go, Chris."

"I'm not letting it go. Was Dad sterile?"

She obfuscated and avoided the issue. She told me in more ways than I'd like to recount how she was never in love with my father, that it was an arranged marriage, that she was unhappy during those years and how she's far happier now that she's free. Hurtful things. I mean, everyone liked my dad, far more people than liked her. She didn't have to work, she didn't have to worry about money, he treated her nicely; he was a good father to me and my sister. Why the misery?

Her only rational answer was that it had to do with her not making the choices herself, being forced into a marriage she did not plan on her own. I imagine I can relate to this, although, knowing the players involved, I disagree with her overall viewpoint. But I was not out to find whether she loved my father or not. I wanted to know who my father *was*.

"I was artificially inseminated. There were problems with your father's sperm. I went to New York City a number of times to get inseminated with your father's sperm. I took the train—I hated driving into the city. It was $75 a shot—the sperm, not the train. I'd have to do it a few times each time I got pregnant, but eventually it took. I got pregnant three times. Three times, three kids."

Well, this was a fine new twist on everything. Of course, at first blush, it made me wonder how this tied in at all with whether or not my father was Al Capone's son. That's how I put it to my Uncle Liam, who I called on again, to verify my mother's version of the artificial insemination story.

"Well, that sounds about right, at least as I've heard it. Just one thing though: that doesn't mean for sure it was your father's sperm. It may have been a donor's, any donor's. Or—and I know they did a bunch of exposés recently about this sort of thing—it may have been the doctor's own sperm. Some of those guys impregnated hundreds of women themselves—

artificially, I mean. I think I saw it on *60 Minutes*."

Oh, great. So now my mother may have been artificially inseminated by Dr. Lots-a-love and I have 400 siblings. Could this get any stranger?

First I checked out the validity of the story in general. Artificial insemination actually dates back to the late 19th century, primarily with livestock. Much of this was science under cloak of secrecy, afraid of governmental and more particularly, religious condemnation. It finally came out of the closet for livestock—mostly cattle—by the mid-1930s.

The first American human born via stored semen was in 1953. Thus, the timeline here works. My older brother was born in 1970, I in 1971, my sister in 1972. My mother claimed each treatment cost $75 per application. This, too, is plausible, or at least in the ballpark. Today, a person would be looking at about $250 per application, and some of that figure is inflated due to the post-AIDS era precautions taken for cleansing the sperm. So, $75 for unclean sperm (my, that sounds unpalatable) in 1970 seems about right. I wonder how monetary inflation affects the sperm market.

The applications are done outpatient, so this also made the train trips to New York City and back in the same day within the realm of possibility. The applications take about 10 minutes and then the woman is encouraged to stay on her back, with her hips elevated, for about another 20 or 30 minutes. Again, it all fits; it's all conceivable (no pun intended).

This brings me back, though, to the syphilis issue—my father wearing a condom when having relations with my mother despite them both wanting children. Congenital syphilis does cause sterility, but sterility has degrees. In most cases, a low sperm count, damaged sperm, or immotile sperm can still be concentrated in a lab setting in order to make it viable where it had not been successful during traditional coitus.

There is also a less-appetizing variation on this: the would-be father with sperm problems allows his sperm to be mixed with another man's sperm (in a lab—they wouldn't have to meet or have a cigarette together afterward). This methodology brings to mind the classic firing squad concept. Six riflemen, five bullets. No man knows for sure if he killed someone or not. In this case, with all those little spermatozoic tadpoles swimming around, there would remain a question as to whose sperm did the deed, if pregnancy were finally successful. Unless, later on, DNA tests were taken. But more on that later.

None of this is relevant, though, if a man is *completely* sterile. Was he? Was my father completely sterile? I have no idea. No matter how my mother may choose to represent it, there is no way, outside of DNA testing, to see for sure whether my sister and I are my father's progeny. The chances of possibly testing my father's sperm died with him. But, like most other aspects of this overall mystery, the strangeness doesn't end there.

My sister and I visited my mother recently. My mom pulled my sister aside and told her, "I want you to go to Trenton State Prison in New Jersey. There's a man there. His name is Jimmy Papadopolous. He's your real father."

Bing, bang, boom.

Seems this Jimmy Papadopolous is in Trenton State

Prison for murder. Back in the early '60s, he was a boarder of my grandmother Dina's, my mother's mother. My mother goes on to tell my sister that she had an affair with Jimmy for a variety of reasons, not the least of which is that she couldn't get pregnant by my father.

This is utter insanity. My sister is distraught beyond words. My mother keeps pushing her and pushing her to go see this man in prison, to visit him and bond with him. Now, as bad a relationship as I have with my mother, my sister's relationship with her is even worse. My sister confides all this in me and I give her a shoulder to cry upon.

Meanwhile, I'm completely screwed up about it myself. First, I have your basic dysfunctional childhood. Then my father dies and I'm told I'm Al Capone's grandson; Al Capone, one of the most notorious gangland murderers who ever lived. Now, I'm told to scuttle that—I'm really the son of a convicted murderer who is still alive and in prison.

Of course, I immediately confronted my mother. "Is Jimmy Papadopolous my real father?"

"No."

"Well then, why did you tell my sister he was?"

"I didn't. I told her that *she* is. You're not."

Oh, like this makes things much better. "Why did you have an affair with a murderer while you were married to Dad?"

The answer was just another litany of how miserable she felt her life was, that she never, ever loved my father and that he was never around for her, blah, blah, blah. So she seduced and bedded a really nice guy…a murderer.

My sister did not want to visit this guy in prison by herself, and asked me to go with her. I wasn't so hot on the idea, either. I mean, I didn't want to leave my sister hanging, but now my mother was claiming he wasn't *my* father, just hers. So why would I want to go visit some strange murderer in a prison? That's a pretty damn upsetting way to spend a day.

My sister resisted and as for myself, I went back to Uncle Liam and asked what he knew about all this.

He winced. "I don't think your mother had what you would call a full-fledged affair with Jimmy Papadopolous. Maybe she slept with him at some point; I don't know. She thinks Jimmy has money. Jimmy was a low-life criminal who did a bunch of robberies. She knows he has money stashed away. Yes, the guy used to live for a while with your grandmother as a boarder, so me and your mother knew him. He's scum. But in addition to the robberies, he also bragged about being from a wealthy family in Greece. He said he had a lot of land there, land worth a lot of money. When your mother heard that, I could see the wheels turning. She's a gold-digger. I hate to say that because she's my half-sister, but it's true. Why do you think she went along with marrying your father? We told her he was Al Capone's son and that he had money. I'm telling you, Christopher, she's just going back to an old well. She figures the guy is locked up for the rest of his life and she's sending your sister in to make friends with him so he might give her some of his money. It's a con job, pure and simple."

I shared this information with my sister, and it quelled her anxieties a bit. No way did she want to trek to some dank, brutal prison and look up some murderer she never saw before in her life, in order to befriend him. But the question remained: was my sister the child of an affair with someone other than

173

my father? For that matter, how much could I invest in my mother's version of things? When Liam mentioned my mother trying to con this con out of money, it was not hard for me to picture. It went along quite nicely with her personality as I'd come to know it.

By then, DNA testing was rising high on my to-do list. DNA could verify or debunk an abundance of theories and queries I had. I had myself tested, and the information logged and catalogued. I encouraged my sister to do the same. When the results came back, one thing was certain: my sister and I were 100 percent brother and sister.

Whew!

So, Jimmy Papadopolous or no Jimmy Papadopolous, if he is the father of one of us, he is the father of both of us. I'm still not sure how much that makes my dreams any sweeter or my sleep more pleasant, but it is what it is. After months of theories and semi-proven hypotheses, finally one thing was certain: I had a real sibling.

Outside of Uncle Liam, though, no other relative or family friend had ever heard of my parents trying to adopt, my mother being artificially inseminated, or her having an affair with a criminal. Perhaps they were being kind, but I pressed them. I'm an adult now; I can handle the truth. But alas, no more information was forthcoming. Most of them were quite taken aback by it all. Poor Chris, always asking these weird questions about his family. Maybe the Navy should be doing psychiatric tests on *him*.

Which finally brings me back to the VA papers and the requests for information as to whether my father would be psychologically fit to be an adoptive parent. The VA's role was not to judge, but to lay the facts on the table. And lay them out they did. My father was still judged as having been last diagnosed as somewhat paranoid and perhaps a bit psychotic. The particulars were consistent with what had previously been written about him—the tales of injuries both real and exacerbated, his feeling that no one thought he was American, *et cetera, et cetera*. All together, they did not paint a beautiful, perfect picture of a potential father. If they'd only had such reports on my *mother!*

Were my parents turned down by adoption agencies? I have no idea. I've grown to distrust my mother so much that I cannot in good conscience go back to her and ask her these sorts of questions, expecting the real truth of any of it. Maybe they were turned down, or maybe the two of them just didn't want to raise the child of a complete stranger. How ironic that is, considering the way my father popped up on the Buzick farm a lifetime ago. Or perhaps it is telling. Maybe for one reason or another, the Buzicks knew *exactly* who Bill Knight was when they first laid eyes on him.

December 26, 1952

To : Veterans Administration
Pass-A-Grille Regional Office
P.O. Box 1437
St. Petersburg, Florida

From : William George Knight
207 East 84th Street
Box 400
New York City, New York

Dear Mr. Parks

Received your letter of October 20,1952 today. In which I was surprise cause there was a letter mail to you on or about Sept. 15, 1952 saying that I wouldn't get to Tampa, Florida until the last of Jannuary in which I would be in Tampa, Florida. I very much wany this examination by the V.A.

Mr. Parks, My mined seem to go and come and having some very bad headake I call them head pains. I take a great deal of aspirin any wher e form twenty to forty a day when my head is giving me trouble.

My wife want to have children. I went to a doctor and he run some test on me and found out that I am impotency unable to produce seamen in which make children. And said this could be cause from my head injury. This is and may break up my home. I am unable to get along with people they say I look like I am mad all the time.

I hope you will be able to continue my disability compensation until the end of the year. My wife is also in bad health andpaying for her and my doctor bills was taking all of my check and some beside. I promise I will be there to take this Physical Examination any time after the 1st. of February. And if I get into Tampa sooner I will drop over and see you. As I stated before I don't get my letter right away. Please allow me time to receive them. Thank You.

Very truly yours,

William George Knight

DEC 30 1925

RECEIVED

Two-Gun Hart

XIV

TWO-GUN HART

There's an old insult: "Why don't you go off and join the circus?" Richard "Two-Gun" Hart took that suggestion literally and left his family at the age of 16, running away from his Brooklyn home and joining a circus in Wichita, Kansas, in 1898.

Two-Gun fell in love with the American West, so much so that he was embarrassed by his Brooklyn accent, choosing instead to pass himself off as either Mexican or Native American, while donning a cowboy hat and developing marksman-like skills with a pair of pearl-handled revolvers, thus earning his nickname. He developed a great love for the wide-open spaces of a part of America that still had thousands of square miles of unsettled, natural beauty. While perhaps it was at first simply a way to enhance his tale of being a Native American, Two-Gun spent time with the Sioux and Cheyenne, learning several Indian languages and developing close relationships with the tribal leaders.

The only relevance this has to my story is that Richard "Two-Gun" Hart was none other than James Vincenzo Capone, Alphonse Capone's oldest brother. I further blurred the issue by neglecting to mention that his accent was most likely equal parts Italian and Brooklynese, having been born in the old country—unlike his brother Al, who was born in the United States.

It would be more dramatic to say that James eschewed his kid brother's name due to the embarrassment Al caused with his life of crime. But, the timeline tells a slightly different tale. James Capone left the family a year before his brother Al was born. Historians chalk it up simply to wanderlust, while I wonder out loud if the family, Al's parents included, had a larcenous streak that made James want to get out at his first opportunity. Remember, Al may have been the godfather, but brothers Ralph, Frank, John, Albert and Matt—all the male Capone siblings except for James—were part of the criminal element as well.

James may have seen it coming, for he not only got away from the Capone family; he cut off all ties with them for the next 30-odd years. You don't do that without good reason, especially if you're the eldest male from an immigrant family. Something was definitely fishy there.

Furthermore, James didn't just go away and do his own thing. His own thing was rather high-minded and downright heroic—the antithesis of how the rest of the family back East turned out. James enlisted in the infantry to fight for his country in World War I, the only Capone to do so. He performed with valor and achieved the rank of lieutenant, serving in France under General John J. Pershing. His family back home in Brooklyn knew nothing about any of this.

Returning to the States, James settled in Homer, Nebraska, and officially changed his name to Richard J. Hart, inspired by a silent film cowboy star with a similar moniker. He married in 1919—around the same time as did his brother Al, who was still a small-time hood in Brooklyn who had not yet achieved the sort of renown that would have reached rural Nebraska.

Just like his brother, January 16, 1920 would be a date that would change his life forever. This was the day when the 18th Amendment to the Constitution of the United States of America took effect—better known as Prohibition. Whereas Al became the boss of bosses, a criminal, entrepreneurial genius who inspired a legacy of gangster films and likenesses, as well as a vast financial empire, James—or, shall we say, "Two-Gun Hart"—became a Prohibition agent. A lawman.

Two-Gun took his job as seriously as his kid brother took his, busting up illegal stills all over Nebraska, usually leading the raids himself, his two pearl-handled revolvers blazing. He became quite the wild West sheriff, so to speak, also chasing down cattle rustlers and assorted criminal types. His fame spread in much the same way as his brother's, albeit in a polar opposite fashion—one became famous, the other, notorious.

Two-Gun was hired by the U.S. Indian Service to keep godless firewater off the reservations. During the summer of 1927, Two-Gun served as a bodyguard for President Calvin Coolidge. If only Silent Cal had known he had put his life in the hands of Scarface Capone's brother!

December 5, 1933 would also have a similarly devastating

effect on Two-Gun's life as it had on Al's. This date marked the *end* of Prohibition. Al was now in jail and Prohibition agents like Two-Gun Hart were no longer necessary. So, he went back to Homer, Nebraska, and his intrepid reputation— still untarnished by any association with the Capone name— procured him the job offer of justice of the peace, regarded as a form of judgeship in the state of Nebraska.

The job paid little and Two-Gun had to scrounge around for other ways to make ends meet. He did odd jobs here and there, but none met the needs of his growing family— he remained married to his first and only wife, Kathleen, and together they had four sons. By 1940, Two-Gun could no longer even afford to pay his electric bill. It was time to swallow his pride and reintroduce himself to the richer side of his family—the criminal side.

Two-Gun reached out to Ralph Capone, who was acting as family patriarch, as Al, freshly out of prison, was riddled with untreated syphilis and unable to function coherently. Ralph and even younger brother John Capone arranged to meet with Two-Gun in Sioux City, Iowa. Then, he went to Chicago to see his mother, Theresa, whom he had not seen or made contact with since he'd run off with the circus at age 16.

When Two-Gun came back home to Nebraska, he was wearing a new suit and had rolls of hundred dollar bills stretching his pockets (shades of Bill Knight). Only then did he tell his loyal wife and their boys that he was in fact Al Capone's brother. At various times from then forward, when financial difficulties beset Two-Gun's family, his brother Ralph helped him out with some more money.

In 1946, a year before he died, Al Capone brought together

his siblings—including Two-Gun—for a family reunion at brother Ralph's famous Mercer, Wisconsin, lodge. Two-Gun brought along his second-eldest son, Harry (his eldest, Richard James Hart, Jr., had recently died serving his country in World War II). Two-Gun told Harry to keep his distance and not get too chummy with Al or Ralph.

Two-Gun was a man conflicted, a person who had gone off to seek his own adventure, fame and fortune while living a clean, upstanding, law-abiding life, yet now he sat at the feet of his criminal brothers, men of far greater wealth and fame, begging for crumbs from their table. How sad; how ironic.

Two-Gun suffered a fatal heart attack in Homer, Nebraska, in 1952. Kathleen and Harry were at his side. His two other boys had settled in Wisconsin, interestingly enough. The final irony to this tale, as it stood during the actual life of Two-Gun, was that his secret identity was finally revealed to the world only a year before his death. In 1951, using his real name of James Vincenzo Capone, he was forced to testify before a grand jury concerning the activities of his brother, Ralph, who was in trouble with the dogged IRS again. Unbeknownst to Two-Gun, Ralph had put the ownership of the Mercer lodge in the name of James Capone. So, Two-Gun Hart/James Capone reluctantly appeared in court and, under oath, lied. At the behest of his brother Ralph, who had given him money when he was in need, Two-Gun returned the favor and told the jury that the lodge was indeed his, thus getting Ralph off the hook.

I can only speculate that, just as Ralph's son had committed suicide shortly after Ralph's appearance before the Kefauver Commission on Organized Crime, this humiliating appearance before a grand jury led to Two-Gun's demise only a year later. An otherwise healthy man in mind, spirit and body, he was only 60 years old at the time of his death.

For me, this tale is almost Shakespearean in the depth of its tragedy. It tells us that crime *does* pay, that the Ralph "Bottles" Capones of the world win in the end and the James "Two-Gun Hart" Capones of the world are saps who end up with nothing, not even their dignity. Had I not been put on this personal journey of mine by Thor, I would not have ever heard this tale, and now that I know it, I weep.

I've seen pictures of Al Capone and some of his brothers. I strain to see the resemblance between them and my father. When I see Al Capone, I see a thick-lipped, round face. My father's face can best be described as long and angular. And then I saw pictures of James "Two-Gun Hart" Capone. And I see my father. The likeness is uncanny. For me, it brought together even more the possibility that my father could be a biological member of this family. And when I look at my own face in the mirror, I see not my father, not Two-Gun Hart, but Big Al Capone.

I have never had brushes with the law. I am a model citizen, a law-abiding person. I am not perfect, not would I care to represent myself as such or be thought of as such. I'm just a normal, everyday guy who works and pays his taxes and doesn't try to hurt anyone.

My father, as I came to know him, was much the same way. Because of what I've recently learned, I wonder today if he was ever "mobbed up," ever associated with organized crime as a way to have the kind of money around that he always seemed to have during my 13 years with him. What exactly did he do on those long truck rides across the country? How were they so lucrative for him? Who staked him the money for those con-vertibles and that string of dry cleaning stores? Was it just Capone family largesse? Certainly, he had no other family, except for some secret family who watched over him. Or did my father have to do something for it, something bad?

If he did, he never got caught. My father's criminal record is spotless, completely non-existent. Or was it simply that he died before it came time to collect? I recall the scene from *The Godfather* where the funeral director asks a favor of Don Corleone and is told, "I will grant you this favor. But remember this: some day, I may need a favor from you. I do not know when or what. But when that time comes, you cannot refuse me, no matter what the favor or what the cost."

That court appearance was Two-Gun Hart's favor, the marker Ralph Capone called in, the returned favor that ruined for Two-Gun a life of independent achievement and respect as a good man, a law-abiding man. He stepped into that witness box, but it was James Capone who stepped down from it. In his obituary only a year later, every other word was Capone, Capone, Capone. The details of his life had been reduced to what criminal he was related to—not who he was, not to the life he had led.

The other day, I found Harry Hart, Two-Gun's son. Harry is well into his 80s now. I told him my tale, told him how I had learned of his father and respected how he had lived his life. Harry was tolerant of me. He still lives in Homer, Nebraska. I find it strange that his two brothers went on to live in Ralph Capone's Wisconsin. Had they left the straight and narrow path their father had blazed for them? I have no idea, nor did I wish to offend Harry with such a question.

What I did ask Harry about was my father. "Nope. Never heard of him. Don't know any Knights. No Bill Knight that I can recall. No woman ever named Knight, either. And I've come to know just about everybody in the family by now. There are no Knights in the Capone family."

"Irene Maude Meis?"

"Nope. Never heard that name, either."

"Myrtle Lillian King? James Buzick?"

It was an exercise in futility. I was throwing name after name at him and nothing was sticking; nothing seemed to cause even a twitter of recognition. Was he lying? Was he covering up? I had no idea. It was over the phone. Perhaps, in person, there would have been those classic visual "tells" the professional poker players are always talking about. But over the phone with this man, a total stranger to me, no, there was nothing at all for me to grasp on to.

"Let me ask you another question: would you be willing to take a DNA test? To see if you and I are related?"

Harry mulled this one over with typical Midwestern slowness and pondering. "Maybe. But if you told anyone the results, I'd have to kill you."

I waited for a chuckle, a late laugh following a pregnant pause, the way a good comedian would deliver such a line. But no laughter or giggle was heard. Harry Hart, son of Two-Gun Hart, the Eliot Ness of Nebraskan Prohibition agents, the son of James Capone, was deadly serious.

I was almost flattered. I'd just had my life threatened by a Capone. How many people walking around today can say that? But that titillating brush with fame only lasted a few moments, for when I got off the phone and went to bed that night, it haunted me. A *real* son of a Capone had just threatened my life. I tossed and turned, sat up and looked around at the familiar shadows of what had once been a relaxing, comforting bedroom. Things were getting uncomfortable.

If I had a DNA sample from Harry Hart, I could prove beyond a shadow of a doubt whether I was a Capone or not. Was it worth the risk to trek on out to Nebraska to get that data? Was he really serious about cooperating? Was he just as serious about keeping the results a secret? It all baffled me.

Al Capone has been dead almost 60 years. I would be happy to sign away any claims I'd have to an estate, if an estate were still accountable. That's the fear I hear in the voices of others who are in or close to the Capone family. "Here comes another gold-digger looking for the old man's money. Like Geraldo breaking into the vault on live television again."

I try to assure them, but trust is hard to earn in millisecond increments. If they got to know me, they'd know I was sincere. But I never get that close. I sometimes manage to blurt out my case, but then the doors get slammed in my face and I'm back to where I started. Is it the paranoia about money? Or is this still some aspect of the *omerta*, the vow of silence, the promise to never, ever snitch? All I want to know is who I am and who my father was.

Announcement! Announcement to all you heirs of Capone! I have no desire to break your code of silence. I have no interest in exposing any secrets of ongoing criminal activities or of those still under investigation or still within the statute of limitations. All I want is to know who I am and who my father was. If he was the son of Al Capone, so be it. If he wasn't, so be it also.

Yes, if he wasn't, I'd still like to know who Bill Knight was, who gave birth to him, and where his roots lie. I would still continue that search. But I have such trouble understanding this silence, this reticence to help me get to the bottom of things. Al Capone murdered people, lots of people. Remember the St. Valentine's Day Massacre? Would it hurt his reputation so much if he were to also be known as a man who had extramarital sex? That's like saying about Hitler, "Oh, and in addition to that Holocaust thing, he also chewed with his mouth open." Please!

But, still, the doors keep slamming; the phones keep getting hung up in my ear. Month after month, year after year, I continue chasing down lead after lead and what does it all add up to? Theories. Theories that are plausible, theories that have validity, theories that may in fact be true or close to true. But in the end, I wish not simply to know who I might be, or who I could be. I want to know who I am. I want to unravel the secrets of my father.

GANGSTER'S WIFE
ONE WHO SUFFERS

Is the First to Learn of Gangland Killing in Chicago, as Cryptic Message Comes to Her.

(Copyright, 1928, by the United Press.)

CHICAGO, July 14.—The gangster's wife, living in constant fear of widowhood, is the first to learn of a gangland killing.

Gangland has its own peculiar way of announcing the death of its members.

The sharp jangle of a bell in the bungalow home of a gangster brings an apprehensive wife to the telephone—it is not time for the regular "all's well" call of the gangster-husband to his wife.

A hoarse voice at the other end of the telephone announces, cryptically:

"Joe's been hurt; he was in an automobile accident. We've got him over here at the city hospital."

"All right, I'll be right over," answers the calm voice in the bungalow.

The gangster's wife knows that at last her fears have been realized —her husband is dead.

In her mind, she probably has gone thru this course of events hundreds of times. Automatically, she prepares to carry thru the "bluff" and goes alone to the hospital.

At the entrance of the hospital, she is met by members of the gang over which her husband ruled. There is no talking. She is accompanied to the morgue and there finds the body of her husband.

The constant fear of death for her husband and its eventual realization is the price the gang leader's wife must pay for the luxury which the wealth and power of her husband affords.

There are few wives who have not tried—some still are trying—to persuade their husbands to "step down" out of the racket, and avoid the certain death which awaits them if they continue.

Gangster Can't Quit

Every influence of home, family and church, which the wife has brought to bear against her husband, has failed, usually because the gangster cannot "step down"— once in, he must "stick."

"Scarface Al" Capone, lord of gangland, admittedly, would like to "step down" and live with his wife and two sons. But he cannot, and so lives in an armored stronghold, while his wife and children dwell in a beautiful bungalow on the Southside, spending perhaps one or two hours during the day with Al.

Mrs Al Capone is surrounded by all that money can buy. However, there is nothing of the show and the display about this quiet Italian wife. She is a "home-woman"; keeps house without servants and is a faithful church-goer. She cannot hide the fear which she holds for Al's life. She, perhaps is the only gang-leader's wife who lives apart from her husband. Others live with their husbands, playing an important part in the protecting ring which gang followers establish around their leaders.

Down on South Justine street lives the wife of "Polack Joe" Saltis, who rose and fell in gangland within a few years. Joe's life is sought constantly by his rivals. He lives at home, seldom venturing outside. Mrs. Saltis, housewife, companion, and bodyguard, is more close-mouthed about her husband's business than Joe himself. She seldom is seen with him and rarely is seen in public places.

The innumerable diamonds which Joe has bought for her usually are replaced by a simple, wide, old-fashioned gold band wedding ring. Her friends are confined to the wives of other members of her husband's gang. Her life is devoted to the comfort of two invalid daughters.

Then there is Marjorie Clemens, widow of the late Hillary "Hetty" Clemens, slain beer salesman of the Ralph Sheldon gang.

Sleepless Many Nights

Marjorie Clemens went sleepless, night after night, waiting, planning and protecting her gangster-husband.

Marjorie is Irish, a dark-haired flapper, and is one of the best known gamblers of gangland. Even now she follows the faro tables, the race tracks and the poker game.

"Hetty" Clemens called Marjorie every half-hour during the time he was out. When his call was five minutes late, Marjorie sent out the call to members of her husband's gang:

"I haven't heard, I haven't heard."

Gangland Plans Welcome Home For Al Capone

'Scarface' Starts Today for Chicago After Completing Sentence in Philadelphia

Life Threatened by Foes

Body Guard Will Accompany Him on Secret Journey

By The United Press

CHICAGO, March 16.—If he isn't slain before he gets here, "Scarface Al" Capone, czar of Chicago's most widely known citizens, · is to have a great homecoming celebration.

If Capone gets out of jail tomorrow in Philadelphia, where he finishes a one-year term for carrying a pistol, he will leave immediately with three bodyguards for the scene of his first triumphs in the liquor and gambling rackets.

Capone should arrive secretly in Chicago some time Tuesday. That night there will be the most elaborate dinner that his friends and relatives can devise.

Relatives Await Return

He probably will get off the train in Indiana and motor to his old home in Prairie Avenue, where his aged mother, his Irish wife and his two young sons have been awaiting his return.

Despite the present danger to Capone, his mother, known to gangland as a "swell cook," is preparing an elaborate Italian dinner for her son. His wife will find a two-fold meaning in the celebration of St. Patrick's birthday tomorrow and his sons are anxious to see their father.

"Jake" Gusick, his spatted and well-barbered chief lieutenant, already has gone to Philadelphia to escort Capone home. "Jake," according to underworld sources, had an excellent report to give his boss. While Capone has been getting fatter and healthier as a file clerk in the Philadelphia jail the faithful "Jake" and all the other members of Capone's "business" organization have been carrying on. Beer trucks have been rumbling through the Loop as usual, according to reports; the various Capone night life resorts have been gay every night and all in all "Scarface" is expected to find his far-flung enterprises in excellent condition.

Capone's Life in Danger

But, if underworld warnings are to be heeded, Capone had better dust off his bullet-proof vest, oil up his armored limousine and see to it that his steel-walled room at the Metropole Hotel is made ready for his use.

"The mob'll let him have his celebration," said the informant, "and then—well, he'd better look out."

Capone's underworld enemies are legion. His autocratic handling of Chicago's rackets, particularly the million-dollar beer business, has been the cause of almost a dozen murders, scores of shootings and general sullenness on the part of gangs not affiliated with that of Capone.

Police said they had no charges to place against the returning gangster chieftain. The Federal government would like to get him behind bars on charges of contempt of court growing out of his income tax troubles. His friends predicted, however, that he would beat the case and that his only worry is the guns of his enemies.

New York Herald 1930

XV

SONNY, RALPHIE AND BILLY

In the *Star Wars* series, Anakin Skywalker's (Darth Vader's) children are kept hidden away so that they will not be killed or led into the evil life of their father. Similarly, Jesus of Nazareth was hidden from the terrors of King Herod, and as a child, wondered if his father was Joseph the carpenter, or God. Grand Duchess Anastasia Nikolaevna of Russia was rumored for years to have escaped execution by Bolshevik troops, living a commoner's life as Anna Anderson, destined to spend a lifetime trying to convince others of her true royal heritage.

Each of these three tales in their own way reminds me of my father and the possible answers to his true lineage. Like Luke Skywalker, was my father hidden away so that the enemies of Al Capone could not get at him? Or was that just the Godfather's way of keeping him from a life of crime alike his own? Similarly, the Jesus of Nazareth story tells of a youth hidden and protected until he was older, and finally able to be told his true identity.

Of the three, the Anastasia story haunts me the most, as it has been far more often conjectured to be a hoax—a young woman, perhaps delusional, perhaps escaped from a mental asylum, simply shows up one day and declares herself a long-lost member of a royal family. Anna Anderson died having never proven, nor really having had disproven, her identity as the ill-fated Anastasia. The more I delve into my father's mystery, the more I fear an Anastasia-like ending.

But then, there is a fourth parallel tale: *The Man in the Iron Mask*. I had grown up assuming it was simply a fairy tale. In the Alexandre Dumas version, King Louis XIV has a twin brother whom he imprisons while he leads a corrupt empire. His twin is not only locked up, but is also forced to wear a mask and is allowed no contact with others for fear his royal heritage and identity may be discovered. The loyal Musketeers uncover this charade, facilitate the jailbreak of Louis' identical twin, and then fight to place him upon the French throne.

I emphasize my assumption that this was all a fictional tale, but have recently come to find that there was indeed a man in an iron mask whose lifelong jailing, masking and cover-up of his true personage has confounded scholars for centuries, as well as inspired the Dumas tale. The more I've delved into Capone lore, the more I've wondered not only who William (Billy) Knight was, but who he was *vis-a-vis* Sonny Capone and even, perhaps, Ralphie Capone.

As with all things, we begin with birth. A child named Sonny Capone was allegedly born December 4, 1918. On December 30, 1918, Al Capone supposedly married Mae

Josephine Coughlin, who was said to be the child's mother. Notice the words "allegedly" and "supposedly"? The truth is, there is very little in the way of proof in so many of these matters. Al Capone had syphilis; we know this because he died of it. If only everything in this adventure were that cut and dried.

A child by the name of Sonny Capone, accompanied by Al Capone, entered a hospital in 1925 with the complaint of a severe ear infection, the type commonly caused by congenital syphilis. This is the only reported incident of a Sonny Capone having a health-related problem potentially due to congenital syphilis. The man who went through his adult life as Sonny Capone went on to live a long and healthy existence, reaching the ripe old age of 85, dying quietly in July of 2004.

Sonny's death, though, contributes to the continuation of the mystery. There is no obituary for Albert Francis "Sonny" Capone. In his later years, he changed his name to simply Albert Francis. I have no record of whether he did this officially, or merely unofficially. But, there is also no obituary for a man named Albert Francis, and there appears to be no death certificate filed anywhere under either the name Albert Francis or Albert Francis Capone. That, of course, is a mystery of greater concern. Sonny was said to have been cremated, thus leaving no easily accessible DNA around for testing.

There is a theory—and it is nothing more than that—that Mae Coughlin Capone never gave birth to any child. If one of the origins of this theory is that had Al had syphilis and passed it along to a child of his, why did Mae not have the same infectious disease? She, too, lived a long and healthy life, surviving to the age of 89, dying in 1986.

I only wish I knew more about congenital syphilis (how often do you hear that in casual conversation?) in order to understand how a person can live with the malady or how long after contracting it a person can go before receiving treatment, and having that treatment work successfully. The question is literally moot today, with the advent of readily available penicillin, unlike when Al Capone died in 1947.

But then, why was my father wearing condoms with my mother in the 1960s and 1970s? One possible answer is that my father was allergic to penicillin. On the other hand, this is a common allergy and there must have been numerous antibiotics in the 1960s that a person allergic to penicillin could have taken instead.

My father, Bill Knight, went on to tell me that he changed his birth date, on his birth certificate, to 1925, in order to appear younger, and that he was really born in 1918. Check that—he said he had a fake birth certificate created on his behalf. Now, no seven-year-old could concoct such a ruse. Nor could any such child execute the plan. This would indicate that someone else, some powerful and well-connected adult, must have thought of and pulled off such a scheme. And no one was more connected in Cook County, Illinois, than Al Capone.

If it were true. My father claimed that both his name as well as his birth date were changed on this new, false document. He claimed it was to gain entrance into the armed services, but this makes no sense, and so I discard it.

My only other working theory is that my father, a ward of the foster care system, pretended to be younger than he was in order to attend public school at the grade level where he belonged. Envision that this was an era when orphans might not have had proper schooling all along the way, and that my father went a few years without getting a formal education and wished to make up for it while living in the stable environment of the Buzick farm.

Yet again, I begin to question and debunk my own theories. Although my father claimed to me and my sister that he had been a part of the foster care system in Illinois, no such record exists for him there. At the same time, almost all records considered mandatory and official today were much more loosey-goosey back then. Maybe he was in that system, and maybe he wasn't.

While I had been operating under the premise that my father arrived on the Buzick farm in 1941, I recently discovered a school photograph of him taken in 1939. It was his freshman high school class in Melvin, Illinois, where the Buzick farm was located. He is identified in the photo as Billy Knight and indeed, it looks for all the world like my father.

The photograph is intriguing. If one were to believe any theories related to my father having been born before 1925, he would have been older than the other kids in the class. The picture is a big group shot and fairly unclear to the naked eye, but one thing stands out: Billy Knight was the tallest kid in the class.

The few readily available pictures of the youthful Sonny Capone are also intriguing. Most of them resemble his father Al quite distinctly. They also favor me frighteningly. They do not resemble my father. A photo I found of first cousin Ralphie Capone is almost like the classic Superman put-on: it simply looks like Sonny Capone wearing eyeglasses. That picture, too, was taken when he was a mere youth. There are few pictures of a grown-up Sonny Capone. Those I've seen do not resemble the old man at all. His face is far more elongated, much more like my own father's face.

In my travels and research, I came across a real Capone expert and aficionado by the name of Mario Gomes. Chatting with Mario, he confirmed his own suspicions of the Sonny photographs: "They look like different people at different times." Now, granted, as none other than Michael Jackson is fond of saying, people's faces do change with age. But we all laughed when Michael said that in defense of his allegation that he's had little to no plastic surgery. In the same spirit, both Mario and I find some of these Sonny photos difficult to explain away to mere maturity and development.

On May 17, 1929, the latter part of Capone's heyday, Al and his bodyguard were arrested in Philadelphia for carrying concealed deadly weapons. Just the day before, they had been in Atlantic City for the very first nationwide Mafia sit-down, an idea formulated by Al's retired predecessor in Chicago, Johnny Torrio, as a way of bringing about greater profits through greater peace among the mobs. Within 16 hours, Al and his bodyguard had been sentenced to terms of one year each. Capone served his time and was released in nine months for good behavior.

An old United Press International story from March 16, 1930 regarding Al's release has probably done more to frighten and excite me than any other Capone clipping I have found. I shall quote: "If he isn't slain before he gets here [Chicago], 'Scarface Al' Capone, czar of Chicago's most widely known citizens [whatever that means], is to have a great homecoming celebration…He probably will get off the train in Indiana and motor to his old home in [sic] Prairie Avenue, where his aged mother, his Irish wife and his two young sons have been awaiting his return."

TWO SONS!

I have to read that over and over again. The phrase repeats itself a little deeper into the article: "Despite the present danger to Capone, his mother, known to gangland as a 'swell cook,' is preparing an elaborate Italian dinner for her son. His wife will find a two-fold meaning in the celebration of St. Patrick's birthday tomorrow and his sons are anxious to see their father."

SONS.

My first reaction was one of pure shock and awe. This is far from the first major newspaper article on Al Capone. By that time he was as much in the public limelight as Lindsay Lohan or Paris Hilton is today. Thus, how could a major news service such as UPI screw up the number of children he had? Granted, the quality of the writing leaves a bit to be desired, but still and all, my research turned up no subsequent retraction.

I have found only one other news source that infers that Al had more than one child. Robert St. John was a reporter for the *Cicero Tribune* back during the time when Al Capone set up shop there. St. John was the classic investigative reporter, always on the lookout for a scoop. He frequently railed against Capone in the *Tribune*, and Al's boys once beat him up badly enough that he had to be hospitalized for it. True to his nature, when it came to dealing both with the press as well as with the average citizenry, Al visited St. John in the hospital and picked up the tab for his doctor's bills.

Mr. St. John led a wonderfully full and interesting life, and lasted to the ripe old age of 101. In an interview with Court TV when he was 98 years young, St. John was asked some banal Al Capone questions geared toward an audience who knew little about the Boss of Bosses. One question was, "How many kids did Al Capone have?"

Mr. St. John's answer: "When he was 19 years old, Capone married an Irish girl named Mae. That was in 1918, when she was 21 he was 19, and *they had a number of children.* Capone liked to pretend that he was a family man. He once said to a young boy who was a member of his family, 'Don't ever become a member of the gang because if you do, I'll kill you.'"

Mr. St. John died in 2003.

My father spoke of living for a time in a wealthy Florida mansion during his youth, prior to the days on the Buzick farm. Was this day, albeit in Chicago, not Florida, one of those days as well?

The article also illuminates the dangers of being Al Capone:

…If underworld warnings are to be heeded, Capone had better dust off his bullet-proof vest, oil up his armored limousine and see to it that his steel-walled room at the Metropole Hotel is made ready for his use.

"The mob'll let him have his celebration," said the informant, "and then—well, he'd better look out."

Capone's underworld enemies are legion. His autocratic handling of Chicago's rackets, particularly the million-dollar beer business, has been the cause of nearly a dozen murders, scores of shootings and general sullenness on the part of gangs not affiliated with that of Capone.

Whew! And I thought some people didn't like the president! But the combination of the two issues in the same article tells a tale I've come to embrace as a possible theory. Capone was always in danger. What more evil way to destroy a man than to destroy that which he loves the most—his family? And the more family there was, the harder it would be to protect them all.

Mention is made of the Metropole Hotel. This was Capone's first major headquarters in Chicago, as he did not wish to imperil his family unduly by conducting his business in his home. Indeed, Capone's room at the Metropole was lined with bulletproof steel. In 1928, he moved his action to the Lexington Hotel, also in Chicago, where decades later Geraldo Rivera would host his ill-fated TV special about Al Capone's secret vault.

But, in all cases, Capone's obsession with security was infinitely prudent. When he went out of town, he rented not only his own hotel room, but the ones above, below, on either side and across the hall. He was always surrounded by armed bodyguards, who stayed in those rooms.

Needless to say, Capone's criminal empire may have been extraordinarily lucrative, but it was not without its overhead expenses. His bodyguards were paid $100 per day—quite the salary in the 1920s. And when out of town, he brought enough men to fill those extra hotel rooms, paying for the rooms, the men and the men's meals. It may sound like fiscal nitpicking, but it begins to add up.

So the issue remains, did Capone have one son or two? Again, all evidence points to only one son, or, shall we say, one *recognized* son. But this, too, can be spun. Perhaps the existence of one son was already "out of the bag"—public information that could not be easily removed from view without staging some elaborate, faked death of said child. If, perhaps, other children followed, the careful and justifiably paranoid criminal mastermind knew to hide them well. Could this have been my father's fate?

If there were indeed a public son and a hidden son (or two), could there have also been a switching back and forth of children for strategic reasons? I wonder. And if so, why? That, I have not been able to figure out yet. Perhaps he sent out a more "expendable" imposter on occasion, if a death threat tip was received? It's possible—cruel and inhuman, but possible. Or, was the mention of a second son simply a misprint? Alas, I do not know. But it is extremely suspicious.

Again, my father's only talk that might lead me to believe he had a life with Al Capone during his childhood was his mention of the Florida mansion. My father's next red flag arose when he once told me he had attended the University of Notre Dame for a time. Sonny Capone also spent one year at Notre Dame. A 1937 group photo of Sonny at the school looks inconclusive—some people look at it and say it resembles the boy of earlier Sonny photographs, while others feel it looks significantly different.

Ralphie Capone also spent a year at Notre Dame, although no pictures appear to be available to record such an occurrence. As for Billy Knight, Notre Dame has no records of any such student by that name. In each case, I find it odd that all three either spent exactly one year at Notre Dame, or claimed to have spent just one year there. Did Notre Dame once have some sort of special one-year-only program? I jest...

But why would my father make such a thing up? As much of a public figure as Al Capone was, by 1937, Sonny Capone had been keeping a low profile for years, and Al had been imprisoned for over 6 years. I highly doubt that Sonny's college matriculation was news, although I could be wrong.

After Notre Dame, Sonny popped up in the news infrequently, his wedding day being a rare exception. In his 1941 wedding photos, he looks nothing like the round-faced child he once was, and everything like my father at the same age. I found another photo, this one of Al and Sonny leaning against a car. These pictures look nothing like the Sonny of earlier pictures, or of Sonny graduating from high school. But, the boy in this particular picture is aged somewhere in between and looks for the life of me like the boy known as Billy Knight in the class photo taken in Melvin, Illinois, in 1939. These are the inconsistencies that Mario the historian and I find maddening.

But one thing is inescapable: there was a man who lived a life as Sonny Capone, just as there was a man who lived the life of Billy Knight. Now, just to debunk the scariest of theories, that Billy and Sonny were one and the same, one man running back and forth, living two concurrent lives, I reach for the dates. Sonny married Diana Ruth Casey in 1941 and in the early '40s, ran a Miami flower shop. In and about that time, Billy Knight showed up on the Buzick farm in Illinois. He lived and worked on the farm and was treated as a son, not as a simple farmhand. There were friends, neighbors and lovers, and none recall Billy Knight scooting back and forth from Florida to Illinois and back. No one re-members Billy disappearing for long periods of time. Billy then entered the Navy in 1942.

Sonny Capone drifted from the public eye of the news

media, but he, or someone playing him, definitely continued to exist. He is said to have kept a low profile, enjoyed his married life with his childhood sweetheart Diana, had children, and been seen at small local public events. He and Diana took up shooting as a hobby, with Diana ironically rumored to have been his superior with a rifle.

Sonny lived in the greater Miami area for decades, or so they say, as did his mother, Mae. Sonny and Mae owned a restaurant there together, named The Grotto. Was this the restaurant that my father was said to have owned when he took my mother on their honeymoon to Florida, when everyone there knew him as a local restaurateur?

The Grotto was a gift from the relics of Al Capone's old mob. It was run at a loss, a front for Mae and Sonny to show as their source of income while they most likely lived on hidden treasures invisible to the feds. The Grotto ran so far into the red that at one point, Momo Giancana was asked to bail Mae and Sonny out of the debts the restaurant created, in the 1960s. Despite the admiration Momo and the Chicago mob still had for Al, and for the old days that had given them the organization they now ran, Giancana was a notorious cheapskate. He told Sonny and Mae to pound sand, a final insult to Al's memory.

And then there was the ill-fated Ralphie, son of Al's closest brother in age, Ralph, Sr. Ralphie committed suicide at age 33 in 1950, after the Kefauver hearings. Or did he? Ralph, Sr., by that time, had continued on a life of crime, albeit nowhere near as successful as that of his brother Alphonse. But after the death of Al in 1947, it was Ralph, Sr. who continued to live on the other side of the law almost continuously, with his Wisconsin lodge and other holdings.

Ralph had no ambitions to battle it out with the new big guys running the Chicago mob, but he had a few things going for himself, and the government knew this well enough to badger him for the rest of his natural life. It was Ralph who was there for brother James "Two-Gun Hart" Capone when Two-Gun fell upon hard financial times. Could it have been that Ralph dished out money to all the down-on-their-luck Capone relatives, including illegitimate children like Billy Knight?

Or was Billy Knight really Ralphie Capone? Did Ralphie really commit suicide, or was that just a ploy for public sympathy, and to get the feds off Ralph's back? In the world of the Capones, almost anything was possible. I've seen pictures of Ralphie and as I mentioned previously, they look exactly like those of Sonny at the same age. But to put a more eerie spin on things, I find no pictures of Ralphie's mother. It is said that she and Ralph, Sr. divorced soon after their marriage and that it was an ugly scene. I can't even find a mention of her name anywhere.

Did Ralph, Sr. really marry? And if so, who? Was Ralphie legitimate? Was Ralph "Bottles" Capone also the illegitimate father of Billy Knight, as opposed to his brother Al, as I'd previously suspected? Along with his infamous Wisconsin lodge, Ralph, Sr. owned another watering hole. He named it "Billy's."

The links and theories between Sonny and Ralphie Capone and my father, Bill Knight, are among the most sensational and intriguing, along with being among the most far-fetched. It is possible that the syphilis issue is somewhat of a red herring, that neither Sonny nor my father's ear troubles had anything to do with congenital syphilis, as that is not the only way one can have such severe mastoid infections. I return to the question of how Al Capone, though, could have had syphilis and not given it to Mae.

Mae was indeed a beautiful, classy woman, a perfect trophy wife for an ambitious man with an eye for public appearances. On the other hand, the fact that Mae was Irish raises questions. In such an era of European immigration, where Italians, Irish, Poles, Jews and many others were ghettoized in their new land, and grew to rival and spat with one another, Capone marrying a non-Italian is puzzling. Indeed, his chief criminal rival in Chicago was Irishman Bugs Moran. Or was his marriage to an Irish girl all a ploy?

Capone was known to have built his criminal empire as quickly and efficiently as he did by aligning with the right people, creating profitable partnerships with disparate warring factions. Of course, in a criminal empire, nothing is perfect, and Capone's rivalry with Moran was proof positive that complete and everlasting peace within such a world, or any world for that matter, was impossible. Was Capone's choice of an Irish woman as his wife a diplomatic move?

If, on the other hand, we were to consider again the syphilis, could it be proof that Mae was indeed merely a trophy wife and that both Sonny and my father were children of prostitutes or loose single women—women Al would have had no qualms about infecting? Did Capone even know that he *had* syphilis during the embryonic days of his sexual activity? So many questions, so many possible answers.

My father once told me his childhood nickname was "Sonny." We had a black Labrador retriever. His name: Sonny.

Giver of the name: my father.

Again, was my father simply an obsessed fan like the enigmatic Thor? Did my father make up many of these tales?

Was he nothing more than a wannabe? Did Thor help plant these ideas in the head of his friend Bill, who could not piece together the youngest years of his life? Together, did Thor and my father feed into each other these wild theories that soon became real to both of them?

Possibly. I only wish that one or both of them were alive today so I could grill them for answers. But how, then, does one explain the money? The gold coins? The convertibles and the cash or credit to start dry cleaning stores and buy trucks? Those things are verifiable and real—I saw many of them with my own two eyes.

Some of my research has even got me thinking like Thor. Sonny liked golf. My father liked golf. Could that mean…? No, there are more than two people in the world who like golf. Furthermore, in life, there are innumerable mere coincidences. But still, my search goes on. I can find no picture of Sonny and Ralphie, close cousins similar in age, together. When I try to contact members of the extended living Capone family, all of them clam up when Sonny's name is mentioned. Mario, the Capone historian, says much the same about his own research.

One day, I decided to post a question on the Internet, asking if anyone knew of Al Capone's TWO sons. I received an almost casual, self-assured response from a man by the name of Vic King. He acted as if the question were well-known to all, that Al Capone's other son was named Lynn. *Oh, my God*, I thought. This, I had to follow up on.

Hooking up with Vic King was as difficult as most of my other adventures. But finally, I tracked him down. And, what ho; Vic King claimed that not only was there a son of Al Capone named Lynn, but that Lynn was *his* father. Vic King was another of Al Capone's long-lost grandchildren!

The Lynn at issue is a Lynn Walter Johnson, who was the son of Julie Jose Johnson. Julie Jose was called Madam Juno back in the day. She used to tell people's fortunes in speakeasies, some of which were owned by Big Al Capone. I ran my DNA against Vic King's. It didn't match. Furthermore, Vic's story, as I checked it, didn't pan out. It was just a family legend passed down. Vic King didn't have proof that his father was Capone's son, although Madam Juno was rumored to have been one of Al's concubines for a time. Apparently, the Lynn Johnson story had been floating around in the ether for ages—unlike mine, where no one I've made contact with has ever heard of a Bill Knight linked to the Capone family. I wonder if that's a good thing or a bad thing.

And so, I am left with more questions than answers. Sonny, Ralphie and Billy. What is their story? Is it Anastasia or is it the man in the iron mask? Are they one, two or three separate people? Did they ever switch roles? Or is my father just another Lynn Johnson? I can only wonder.

Gabby Hartnett, Al Capone with a young boy Sam Pontarelli

Al Capone and Son

Al Capone and Son

Me at 24 years old

XVI

BACK TO ME

Al Capone, Ralph Capone, Two-Gun Hart. Sonny Capone, Ralphie Capone, Billy Knight. All dead. All gone. But I'm still here.

I am neither famous nor infamous. I find it strange sometimes, thinking about what I've thrown myself into. But in immersing myself in the lives of others, many of whom I have never met and shall never meet, I find similarities to myself and my own life experiences. Empathy, I believe they call it. But in my case, it has also been an exercise in studying human nature and then taking a hard look in the mirror, and examining myself and my personal history through a different prism.

After my father died, my mother went a different kind of crazy. I mean, different for her. The verbal abuse continued, but the physical died down. That was replaced by neglect. My mother took some of my father's money (I suppose) and went away on European vacations for three or four months at a time, while my sister and I sat at home. Sometimes, we were left with enough money to make ends meet and feed ourselves. Often, we were not. My sister used to hock her jewelry for food.

As I previously mentioned, Mrs. Labue, the coolest lady in Brooklyn, frequently swooped in and saved us. She, too, has now passed on. But as un-famous as she was compared to other people mentioned in this book, she is nonetheless as much as an enigma as they.

This woman was not a relative. I cannot recall my sister or me calling and pestering her when our mother pulled some of her typical shenanigans. And yet, still, she was there, like someone had lit up the Bat-signal, telling her to hop in her Iroc Z as if it were her own personal Batmobile, and get herself to Jersey. She was not poor. If she received any money at all from my mother, it was a pittance. My impression was that she was never paid at all for her services, nor did she *need* the money.

So why, if not a relative and not for pay, would she do it? I have no idea. She was older than my mother, much closer to my father's age. Furthermore, she hated my mother immensely. My sister and I were often without proper shoes. Then, Mrs. Labue would appear. Off we'd go to the shoe store, and not just any shoe store for any old pair of cheap shoes. "Motherfucking shoes don't tear, 'cause motherfucker doesn't care." Transla-tion: "Good shoes were worth the price." But the colorful lingo gives you a beacon into the world of Mrs. Labue.

She was Italian, while my mother was not and my father... Well, we never quite knew *what* he was. And today, I'm not quite exactly sure *who* he was. But it goes without saying that

Al Capone was Italian as well. One hundred percent Italian, as was Mrs. Labue. While I can't recall her saying it to my mother's face, Mrs. Labue often preferred to refer to my mother as *puttana*—Italian for "cheap, gold-digging whore" (or something equally colorful, depending upon your preferred English translation).

It stands to reason that now, looking back, I am amazed that I took Mrs. Labue's existence at face value. I mean, how many people have now or did have someone like her in their lives? Someone who lived miles away, was not a relative, was not paid to help, who just knew to come on by when things were at their worst, and protect two children? And why, why, why?

But Mrs. Labue or no Mrs. Labue, my sister and I grew up traumatized and damaged, managing to function today, thank you, but still considered works-in-progress. Both of us suffer from low self-esteem. According to our mother, everything either of us ever did was wrong, or done wrong.

My sister is married and has three kids. Her husband is, ironically, a truck driver. He loves her and sticks by her, and she is blessed to have him in her life. As a mother herself, she is, for lack of a better word, confused. This is not to say that she is a bad mother—heaven forbid; she is a thousand times the mother that our mother was. But, she struggles with the responsibilities of parenting, and I feel for her. It's hard when you've had no positive mothering models in your life.

For me, when it comes to parenting, it's less likely to be an issue. I happen to be gay. Like most gay, lesbian or transgendered people, coming to terms with my sexuality and establishing my true self within my family was not easy. Of course, this, too, was exacerbated by my mother's insanity. I can still vividly recall her chasing me around the dining room table when I was about 16, calling me a "God damn faggot." Not a pretty scene. She harassed, she badgered, she abused. Somehow, though, I got through.

Obviously, getting out of our house at the first possible opportunity would sound like a logical plan. But, one has to understand the mentality of an abused person. I was stripped of my dignity, completely lacking in self-confidence. I was afraid to have dreams because my mother would only latch onto them as a new topic to discuss with pure derision. "You'll fail, Chris. You always fail." Thus, for as much as college would seem to be a wise choice in order to establish myself as a fully actualized and sane survivor, I had no confidence that I could do it.

This began while I was still in high school and only imagining what the future held for me. My senior year, I hardly ever attended class. I still have no idea how or why they let me graduate. I know it got so bad that my mother even got involved. Now, for as much as the woman deviled me, she did not want to see me *publicly* embarrassed. That would also embarrass *her*. Life with my mother was about the illusions of status. My sister and I were a part of that public facade.

So, despite my mental anxieties that kept me from being able to function in a high school classroom, on graduation day, I was still handed a diploma. Did my mother sleep with the superintendent of schools? I have no idea. But insofar as the typical requirements for graduation, I did not properly earn them.

Again, this would have seemed like the perfect time to escape, to run as far from this woman as possible. And yet, because of how poorly she parented me, I could not. No confidence. Stockholm Syndrome—the prisoner learning to latch onto and relate to his captor to such a degree that locked doors are no longer necessary, despite the abuse and the obvious logic of needing and wanting to get away. A real catch-22. Instead of bolting for freedom, my first year out of high school was spent working in a grocery store and living at home.

The following year, I finally got my act together enough to apply to Rider University, a short drive from where we lived in New Jersey. Incredibly, they accepted me. None of this is to infer that I was dumb or a poor student. But, attendance is a basic to success at anything.

Despite how my mother withheld money as much as she withheld love, college was something she somehow managed to afford. This was because of the "trophy baby syndrome." If you have kids, they must attend and graduate college. It's simply the norm. Anything less in white, middle-class America is simply déclassé. And so, to keep up public images, mother paid the college tuition bill.

College was at times a respite, but as most students or former students know, the umbilical cord is still attached until a person is out of college and earning all of their money on their own. Money was indeed the issue. At times, she threw it at my sister and me like a drunken sailor. At other times, at the most bizarre times, she raged at us for daring to want to, oh...eat?

Living in the dorms at Rider, I would sometimes let other guys on my hall listen to my mother throw conniptions at me over the phone. "See, you thought I was exaggerating about her." They would leave shaking their heads in amazement.

But college still had its share of good times. I had been overweight as a child, but instead of gaining the famed "freshman 15," I actually lost 80 pounds during my college career. This had a positive effect on my social life, thank God. Other things went well, too. Mom's irate phone calls aside, I was secluded enough away from my mother that I was able to gather up the courage and ambition to attend classes, and did so well that I was able to complete my undergrad degree in only three-and-a-half years, and maintain a very good GPA.

Despite the nearness of our home, in Jersey City, New Jersey, to Rider University in Princeton, and the fact that Rider was somewhat of a "suitcase school"—with many of the students being local to the area and heading back home most weekends—continuing to live with my mother was out of the question. This attitude continued even after college. I got my first job right in the same locale, and rented a room in Princeton for $300 a month. It wasn't much, but it was mine. And, no one ruled it but me. Freedom at last!

I lasted one year. I had a degree in accounting, but I was woefully unprepared for the real world workplace both professionally and emotionally. I got fired, and I deserved to get fired. Self-confidence—I had none of it. I bumbled and mumbled my way through my work day, wondering what the hell I was doing, assuming I had no right to the job, assuming I could not learn to do anything I did not already know (which was, in my opinion, very little). This sort of losing, victimized attitude would haunt me for years.

Jobless, the thought of moving back in with my mother seemed like a fate worse than death. She must have been in agreement. She started sending me money, enough to continue to live on my own. Love? Compassion? No. She simply made it clear to me that I was no longer welcome under her roof.

I had to get out of there. I was so close to home that, despite my mother literally barring the door, there was the chance that I would go crawling back home if I didn't put more physical distance between myself and her. I decided to move to Boston and attend grad school at Suffolk University.

My mother continued her financial schizophrenia by tossing some money at me so that I could continue my studies. It wasn't much, but I made it work. I found the world's worst apartment in Roxbury, the most crime-ridden neighborhood in Boston. The apartment was small, the neighborhood was like a bad B-movie, and yet somehow, I came to regard it as home. Outside my building were hookers and junkies. After a while, we came to know each other by name. Funny how that is. Even street people become neighborly once you get to know them.

Boston gave me a bit more perspective, a bit more of an opportunity to breathe and grow. God knows I needed it. While I was in Boston, my sister remained in New Jersey. As much as I complain, I think she had it worse with my mother—or maybe it was simply the differences in our genders or our personalities. Mothers and daughters are supposed to have a special bond. My sister had none of that and without being able to enunciate it as such, found herself even more miserable and ineffectual in the world.

It's funny, but when I go through the morass of my father's VA documents, I find correspondence from my mother to the VA from around that time period. The poor, aggrieved widow Knight. "My husband died with nothing but debts and I have two children who are both in college. Help me! Help me!" She always neglected to mention the safe deposit box with the gold bullion, or the wads of cash my father seemed to have left everywhere. So, maybe the money she helped me out with was not even really hers, but money the government owed my father for the educational benefit of his children. Whatever...

My first job after grad school lasted three months. It appeared that I was getting worse at the employment game, rather than better. The year was 1998. One evening, I was standing outside a bar, smoking a cigarette, when I saw these guys moving furniture into an office building late at night. They didn't appear to be professional movers, just normal, everyday guys like me. I'm the friendly, talkative sort, so I began chatting them up. "What are you doing? Why are you moving furniture this late at night?"

Their story was that they were an Internet start-up company and couldn't afford professional movers. The more I talked with them about their company and their aspirations, the more excited I became. I loved being around positive people, people without the emotional baggage I seemed to never be able to rid myself of.

"Look, I'm an accountant. If you're hiring, I'd love to get involved with you. I'm available."

They took me up on my offer. I was hired as one of their original 10 employees. They gave me an impressive-sounding title, and I worked my little fingers to the bone. Everyone else there did, too. The atmosphere was wonderful, and I began to blossom as I never had before.

The company blossomed as well, and soon I had 45 people working under me. Me, the guy who couldn't hold a job before, who couldn't get it together enough to get out of bed and go to high school. I was the chief accountant of a $350 million company. I was suddenly a success.

The part where I volunteered to "get involved" and said that I was "available" was meant on more than one level as well. The company's president was also gay, and we developed a platonic relationship. It was wonderful. *He* was wonderful, and still is. Unfortunately, he and the company became as successful as they did because he was a driven workaholic. I suppose most successful people are, but it makes it tough on relationships.

Still, he and the career he provided me gradually gave me confidence and, for the first time in my life, stability. Even my father couldn't really give me that, not with his own form of workaholism—his week-long trips out of town, leaving me behind with my monster mother.

I also made more and more friends. This was something I'd always wanted, but even there, too, my mother had made it almost impossible when I was younger. She had a tall metal fence built around our yard and my sister and I could never go outside its gates. Other kids would come by and we'd play together—through the fence. Such an odd existence. It's a wonder I function as well as I do today. I can still recall poking my fingers through the prison bars of that fence so I could actually experience the human touch of another child. So pathetic, so wrong.

During all those years, I could not conceive of getting my head together enough to sit and rationally think about my father and his secrets. I needed the time to figure myself out, to find a place in the world where I could stretch my legs and walk on my own, and to travel down my own path. If you were wondering why so much time passed between when I spoke to Thor, shortly after my father's death, when he put me on to the whole Capone thing, and now, when I am pursuing it, that's the reason in a nutshell. It took that much time, but once it happened, I was finally able to be where I am today—trying to put it all in context and trying to piece together the backstory of my life. Who am I? What part of my make-up is nature and what part is (lack of) nurture?

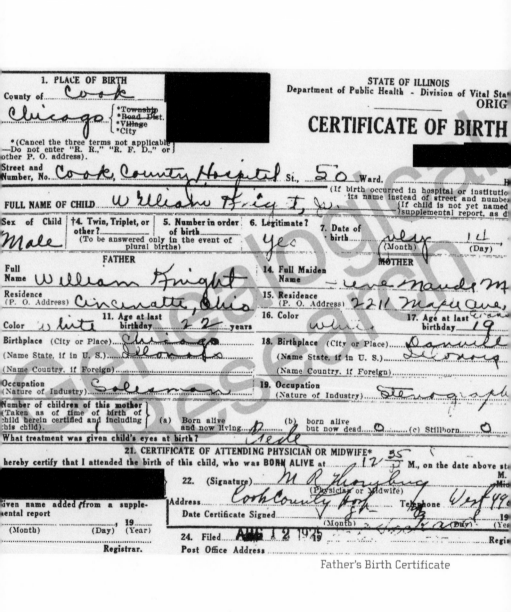

1. PLACE OF BIRTH

County of _Cook_

Chicago {
- *Township
- *Road Dist.
- *Village
- *City

*(Cancel the three terms not applicable)
—Do not enter "R. R.," "R. F. D.," or other P. O. address).

STATE OF ILLINOIS
Department of Public Health - Division of Vital Sta___
ORIG___

CERTIFICATE OF BIRTH

Street and Number, No. _Cook County Hospital_ St., _50_ Ward.
(If birth occurred in hospital or institution its name instead of street and number
(If child is not yet named
(supplemental report, as di___

FULL NAME OF CHILD _William Krig I, Jr._

Sex of Child _Male_	†4. Twin, Triplet, or other? (To be answered only in the event of plural births)	5. Number in order of birth	6. Legitimate? _Yes_	7. Date of birth _July_ (Month) _14_ (Day)

FATHER

Full Name _William Knight_

Residence (P. O. Address) _Cincinatte, Ohio_

Color _white_   11. Age at last birthday _22_ years

Birthplace (City or Place) _Chicago_
(Name State, if in U. S.) _Illinois_
(Name Country, if Foreign)

Occupation (Nature of Industry) _Salesman_

MOTHER

14. Full Maiden Name _Eve Maude M___

15. Residence (P. O. Address) _2211 Maple Ave._

16. Color _white_   17. Age at last birthday _19_

18. Birthplace (City or Place) _Danville_
(Name State, if in U. S.) _Illinois_
(Name Country, if Foreign)

19. Occupation (Nature of Industry) _Stenographe___

Number of children of this mother (Taken as of time of birth of child herein certified and including this child).
(a) Born alive and now living _1_   (b) born alive but now dead _0_   (c) Stillborn _0_

What treatment was given child's eyes at birth? _None_

21. CERTIFICATE OF ATTENDING PHYSICIAN OR MIDWIFE*

hereby certify that I attended the birth of this child, who was BORN ALIVE at _12 35_ M., on the date above sta___ M.

22. (Signature) _M R Thornburg_
(Physician or Midwife)   Mid___

Address _Cook County Hosp._   Telephone _West 49___

Date Certificate Signed _____ (Month) _____ (Day) _____ 19___

given name added from a supplemental report

_____, 19___
(Month) (Day) (Year)

_____ Registrar.

24. Filed _AUG 12 1925_ 19___   Regis___

Post Office Address _____

Father's Birth Certificate

XVII

BLOOD

God bless the Internet. I should send Al Gore, or whoever invented it, a Valentine every year. The Internet has become my greatest investigative tool as I amble along the world's invisible highways of words, thoughts, facts and remembrances. It is my primary source for leads, both direct and oblique, as I attempt to find out more about my father and my true lineage.

A few months ago, I came in contact with a grandchild of Ralph Capone. Ralphie (Ralph Jr.) was not her father, but her mother was Ralph, Sr.'s daughter. She, too, had an abiding interest genealogy.

As we cyber-chatted, I felt I'd met a kindred spirit. While almost all of the other Capone family members I'd come across had slammed doors in my face, Colleen was willing to become a friend to me. One of the first practical things she brought to my attention was that if my father's tale of being sired by Al Capone in 1917 or 1918 were true, then he would have been born in New York, not Cook County, Illinois. Al Capone himself didn't get to Illinois until well into 1919. That still left open the possibility that my father was, indeed, born during one of those years, but that in addition to a Cook County birth certificate being created in 1925, there would also most likely have been a New York certificate from 1917 or 1918 that was destroyed.

The other pertinent things that Colleen shared with me were her knowledge of Al Capone's genetic traits. His blood type was O. Capone and many of his siblings were heavy drinkers, quick and violent tempered, sexually unfaithful and socially immature.

In my haste to associate myself with this charismatic enigma of American folklore and history, I had allowed myself to gloss over the most negative aspects of Al Capone's life. Desiring to neatly wrap up a package of claiming him as my grandfather, the father to my father, I had focused far more on his fame, his social charitableness and his positive public relations gestures. But the "Scarface" that even his living family members avoid discussing was as violent as the bloody movie bearing his infamous moniker, remade in 1983, starring Al Pacino, a favorite of every thug gangsta rapper in the music business.

The seamy underside of Al Capone started out as a life full of good intentions. He was not, as rumor has it, born in Italy, but was a native-born American. His parents worked hard and he had, considering their poverty, a decent, traditional upbringing. All indications point to the theory that Al was not genetically predisposed toward a criminal life, but was more a victim of destitution and desperation, growing up near the old Brooklyn Navy Yard in a cold-water flat with no indoor plumbing. Crime ran rampant in those parts, as drunken sailors patrolled the streets in search of all things illegal and immoral.

Al only managed a sixth grade education, having been beaten up by his school principal for beating up his teacher (I suppose that was how things of that nature were dealt with in that time and place). Prior to that, though, he was already running around in street gangs, considered somewhat of a mascot of the Navy Street Boys gang, run by, ironically, the older Frank Nitto, the man who would someday replace Capone as head of the Chicago mob that Al built into a criminal empire. Other full-fledged members of the Navy Street Boys were Al's older brothers Ralph, Frank and even straightedge James (Two-Gun Hart), although James would eventually drift away from both the Capone family and criminal elements in general.

From the Navy Street Boys, Al eventually graduated to the James Street Gang, led by the man who would become his *real* Godfather, Johnny Torrio, who would also be the person actually to start the modern Chicago underworld—not Al, as most people assume. The James Streeters also included the soon-to-be-notorious Lucky Luciano, who is considered the true father of modern organized crime. His specialties included an eventual complete control of all New York houses of prostitution, and the introduction of the modern heroin trade, an empire that lives on today. It was Luciano who was to lay down the edict that "we only kill each other," meaning that mobsters should shy away from the killing of average citizens. Despite this, Luciano is credited with killing or ordering the murders of at least 500 men.

rom the James Street Gang, young Al drifted into the ~~~~ Brooklyn Rippers (such lovely names), and finally the 40 Thieves Juniors, a youthful derivative of the notorious Five-Points Gang. The bloody Five-Points neighborhood and its criminal element were recently captured in Martin Scorsese's fine film *Gangs of New York*.

The 40 Thieves were led by Frankie Yale, the man credited with truly introducing Alphonse to a life of violent crime. Yale owned a bar named, ironically, the Harvard Inn, on Coney Island. He employed the teenage Capone as an underage bartender, not that anyone dared to investigate the legality of it. Al's age was the least of the larcenous activities going on in and around the Harvard Inn.

Yale, like Al who would follow in his footsteps, tried to present a pleasant front to the world at large, but behind his jovial veneer was the heart of a madman killer. His chief executioner was a man named Willie "Two-Knife" Altierri. Two-Knife's moniker was cooked up due to his signature murdering style—sticking two knives deeply into a victim's gut, then breaking off their handles. Yale would then mount the handles over the desk in his office, a trophy and a warning to all who viewed them.

One night, while bartending at the Harvard Inn, Al paid what he thought was a compliment to a young lady who had entered with her older brother, mobster Frank Galluccio. Al said, "You have a beautiful ass, and I mean that as a compliment, really, I do." Galluccio asked for an apology and when none was forthcoming, pulled out a knife and deeply sliced Capone's cheek, creating his infamous scar. Later, Yale, Galluccio, Capone and Lucky Luciano had a sit-down to straighten things out. It was agreed that Al would apologize for the vulgar insult to Galluccio's sister, and that Galluccio would pay Capone $1000 for his troubles.

During his time at the Harvard Inn, it is said that teenage Al committed two murders at the behest of Frankie Yale. I find it strange and appalling that life could be considered so cheap and insignificant that the deaths of two human beings could be chronicled so cavalierly. These men had mothers and fathers, probably sisters and brothers. Did they deserve to die? Who is to say? And if so, were they given any sort of due process? Of course not. This was mob justice and mob warfare. It was survival of the fittest, with fitness judged mostly on raw, brute strength and the greatest lack of civil restraint.

Yale's biggest organized crime rival was "Wild Bill" Lovett and his White Hand Gang. The White Handers were Irish, while Yale, Capone, Luciano, *et al*, were Italian. Ethnic gangs were the norm, with Irish and Italians being among the most bitter rivals, while numerous Jews and blacks either formed their own gangs that worked in peaceful concert with the more powerful and vicious Irish and Italians, or joined them outright.

Due to the rivalry between Yale and the White Hand Gang, Yale's boys soon became known as the Black Hand Gang, but not of their own volition, although the phrase "the black hand" was common among true Sicilian Mafioso, dating back to the mid-1700s. Both Yale and Capone were Neapolitan.

By that time, a particular criminal specialty of Capone's was loan sharking on behalf of his mentor, Yale. Once, while out collecting for Yale, Al engaged in brutal fisticuffs with a

White Hander by the name of "Criss-Cross" Finnegan, nearly beating the man to death. Capone went on the lam, hiding out, abetted by his patron, Frankie Yale.

But, the animosity between the two gangs was not something that would soon blow away. Indeed, they would skirmish on into the mid to late 1920s. Wild Bill Lovett was ravenously on the prowl for "the scarred man"—the only description of Capone—who had nearly killed his man, Criss-Cross.

A few years earlier, Johnny Torrio, Frankie Yale's mentor, had moved on to Chicago at the behest of his uncle, "Big Jim" Colosimo, a small-time pimp who had, ironically, been threatened by Sicilians who proudly referred to themselves as Black Handers. With the vicious Johnny "The Fox" Torrio at his right hand, Big Jim struck back hard and soon became one of Chicago's first big crime bosses.

Things were good for Torrio and his uncle until the advent of Prohibition. Big Jim wanted little to do with the new enterprise, fearing it would draw too much attention and make him more of a mark for the police. Torrio was frustrated.

Yale contacted Torrio and asked that he do him a favor by taking on his protégé, Al Capone, and moving him to the safety of Chicago. But for Torrio, there would be a *quid pro quo*. Torrio wanted his uncle, Big Jim, out of the way. For years, it has been surmised that Yale himself came to Chicago to rub out Big Jim Colosimo, although no arrests were ever made in this murder, which involved two bullets to Colosimo's head as he stood helplessly in the vestibule of one of his brothels—waiting, ironically, for a delivery of illegal whiskey.

Decades later, FBI wiretaps would reveal that Colosimo's murderer was, in fact, Al Capone. Thus, by the tender age of 21, Capone had already been fingered for at least three cold-blooded murders—ones not ordered by him, as would be his wont years later, when he himself became a crime boss—but murders committed by his own hand.

I think of myself at 21. I think of the dysfunction of my childhood, the craziness of my mother, the taunting of my schoolmates, and I wonder if I ever felt that I could kill someone. The answer is no. This is not to say that I do not understand rage. I also believe that every human being has within themselves the potential to kill under the right circumstances. To take a less sinister view of this opinion, simply look at military service during wartime, particularly during the times of military drafts and mandatory conscription, when many normal, peaceful, law-abiding men are handed guns and taught to shoot other men.

As we Americans discuss war today, it is with a detachment that an all-volunteer Army affords us. Every day, I hear people saying, "We should nuke the bastards," or, "We should send more troops to kill those (insert name of foreign group we do not like here)." Somehow, I feel that the national discussion would be somewhat different were everyone who said such things expected to pick up a gun and do it themselves, while, of course, attempting to dodge the bullets of an enemy who felt the same way about them.

But, Al Capone was not about war and politics. He was about urban survival. Unfortunately, his became a life driven by greed far beyond the pale. He was not a white-collar Wall Streeter engaged in insider trading. When he became intracta-

bly ensconced in the world of gangs, and of Frankie Yale and
Johnny Torrio, he was training to be a barber. Imagine a nice,
young Italian boy, born in America to immigrant parents,
learning a trade that might allow him someday to start his own
business and become an upstanding, law-abiding member of
the community. Would his have been true wealth? No,
probably not. But it could have led to a comfortable, middle-
class life, where he might have been able to move his family to
a safer neighborhood, raise a family, give them moral values,
and pass that torch along to his own children as a model for
their future lives.

Instead, there was greed for far more, and obviously, a lack
of basic morality that condoned the sort of rage that found
murder acceptable, if for a strategic or vengeful, egotistical,
macho reasons.

Torrio now ran Chicago, with Al Capone at his side. The
corrupt Chicago mayor, "Big Bill" Thompson, had turned a blind
eye (and a waiting palm) to organized crime in the city. But
when Thompson was replaced by reformer William E. Dever,
things changed. For one thing, Capone's foray into Cicero,
Illinois, began. All was good with the Capone takeover of Cicero,
aided by his own brothers, whom he had by now brought along
with him to the Midwest, with the obvious exception of
independent-minded Two-Gun Hart. Al brought his mother to
Illinois as well, his father having passed away in 1920.

When the infamous Cicero election came and Capone
sought to "legally" take over the city, much the way that Adolph
Hitler was elected chancellor of Germany, violence ruled the
streets, with Capone's thugs tossing people out of polling
places if it was felt that they were not supporters of Big Al's

candidates. Physical violence and voter intimidation got so bad that Chicago's Mayor Dever sent 70 armed policemen down to Cicero, to quell the uprising.

On the lookout for Capone and his henchmen, the police came upon Capone's brother Frank as he strolled innocently down the street, unarmed. Police gunned Frank down, Amadou Diallo-style, riddling his body with bullets. No charges were filed, and just as in the more recent Diallo case in New York, during the Giuliani administration, the police claimed self-defense (against an unarmed victim).

Al was crushed. He escalated the election day violence, turning up the heat to such a point that at least one election official was murdered on his behalf. After the smoke had cleared and Capone's slate of candidates had won, Al threw brother Frank a hero's funeral, but he remained inconsolable. This may have been the low point in Al's life, his last turning point where he could have thrown it all in and changed his ways.

But, it was not to be. It is said that Al contemplated going into armed warfare with the Chicago police, as Mayor Dever had the nerve to send the same cops to Cicero for Frank Capone's funeral. This became the premise for the pop song "The Night Chicago Died" by Paper Lace, recorded in the 1970s, erroneously assumed by many to have been based on true events, not speculated ones, as were the facts of the case.

Indeed, despite what many have learned from television, books and movies about the inability to "leave" the Mafia, many chieftains did. The name Dion O'Banion plays a large role in the Chicago mob wars of the early 1920s. The Irish O'Banion was Torrio's and Capone's chief rival, running Chicago's North

Side while the Italians ran the city's South Side. Despite this, O'Banion personally paid for $20,000 worth of flowers for Frank Capone's funeral (1920s dollars).

This did little to quell the animosity between the rival gangs. Murders and beatings continued between "soldiers" in both camps before Torrio finally ordered O'Banion's murder, carried out by none other than good old Frankie Yale of New York, continuing Torrio's and Yale's string of reciprocal, bloody murders. Yale, by this time, had taken another young gangster under his wing—the soon-to-be-notorious Albert Anastasia, creator of Murder Incorporated, the first Mafia crew whose primary business was murder-for-hire.

Anastasia would eventually be credited with at least 700 murders, many committed by his own hand. In a power play, he was eventually murdered while sitting in a barber chair, his face and eyes covered with a hot, moist towel, a scene cinematically recreated in many mob movies.

Yale also sent another young man to Chicago to apprentice under Capone, in much the same way that he sent Capone for protection under Johnny Torrio's wing: "Machine Gun" McGurn. His name may have sounded Irish, but he was really an Italian named Vincenzo Gibaldi, and he became one of Al Capone's most trusted henchmen.

Soon after, O'Banion's boys attempted to kill Torrio and nearly succeeded. Bullets were pumped into Torrio's car and body. The raid was lead by O'Banion's successor, "Bugs" Moran, who was to become Capone's chief nemesis until the end of his days. After doing significant damage, Moran walked up to Torrio's stopped car, placed his gun to Torrio's head, and fired. Nothing. Moran was out of bullets.

While recovering in the hospital, Torrio finally saw the light. He turned to Capone and said, "Al, it's all yours." When Torrio felt healthy enough, he moved to Italy with his wife and mother, retiring from organized crime, alive and relatively young and healthy.

A few weeks after the Cicero election, Al, still an emotional wreck, ran into a small-time thug by the name of Joe Howard, who asked for a loan, and Al turned him down. Howard responded by calling Al a dago pimp—in public. Bad move. Al pulled out a revolver and shot Howard dead on the spot.

Prosecutors finally felt they had Capone where they wanted him, but it was not to be, as all eyewitnesses to the Howard murder suddenly developed hazy memories and even hazier eyesight. Al walked.

Back in New York, Frankie Yale's disputes with the Irish White Hand Gang were nearly over, becoming more nuisance than competition. Nonetheless, a wounded animal is a dangerous animal, and these men were all animals. The day after Christmas, 1925, Al Capone was visiting Yale in New York while taking his son Sonny to doctors regarding his ear. By then, the White Handers were headed by a man named Pegleg Lonergan, Wild Bill Lovett having been killed while lying in a drunken stupor, accidentally discovered that way by a crew led by Yale's executioner, Two-Knife Altierri. Lovett took a meat cleaver to the head, and was a nuisance no more.

Lonergan decided to make one last offensive against Yale. On December 26, 1925, Lonergan brought a gang with him to Yale's Adonis Club. Yale, presumably, had been tipped off in advance. Lonergan and his boys took a table and waited for the right moment. After a few drinks, they stood up and whipped out their guns. Immediately, all the lights in the club went out except for one directly above Lonergan's table. Al Capone personally headed a firing squad that wiped out Lon-ergan and his men, with the exception of one poor soul who staggered outside, only to have his head split open with a meat cleaver, a popular form of murder-with-a-message, courtesy of Frankie Yale. The White Hand Gang was finished.

Even the best of friends within the criminal world eventually turned on one another, for one reason or another. Certainly, no two people seemed closer than Al Capone and Frankie Yale, yet they, too, would find conflict. Yale had asked that a pal of his be placed in a high, mob-backed union position. Capone went a different way. Yale was supposed to provide protection for Capone's bootlegging trucks as they rambled through New York. Trucks began getting lighter and lighter in their loads, and some were out-and-out highjacked. Capone sent a trusted associate to investigate. The associate fingered Yale as ripping off his old employee, Capone, and turned up dead a few days later in Brooklyn.

As much as it tore him up inside, Capone was no longer in a position to allow such betrayal to go on without appearing weak and vulnerable. He sent a four-man team to Brooklyn and lured Frankie Yale out of one of his clubs by having someone call and claim that Yale's wife was in peril. Yale bolted outside and jumped in his car. At the first traffic light he encountered, an ominous car pulled up alongside him. Figuring this looked like trouble, Yale peeled out, the other car in hot pursuit.

The car with Capone's men finally caught up with Yale's car and filled it with machine-gun fire and shotgun shells. Yale, dead at the wheel, spun out of control and crashed into a building where a Bar Mitzvah was in progress.

The Frankie Yale hit was the first time the tommy gun had been used in a New York murder. Al was questioned intensely about the crime, but there was no solid evidence to hold him. The four triggermen were Fred "Killer" Burke, Gus Winkler, George "Shotgun" Ziegler and Louis "Little New York" Campagna, most of whom would participate in the St. Valentine's Day Massacre seven months later. Ballistics would eventually trace one of the tommy guns used in the Massacre to Yale's murder.

With Torrio retired and Yale murdered on his own orders, Al Capone was now a man in charge of his own destiny. A young man at that—at his peak of power, he was still only in his 20s, an amazing feat. And yet, this is all the more frightening. Excessive violence, raw hatred and a carnality toward bloodshed is most often the province of the young, those driven by hormonal rages, possessing a feeling of invincibility and bearing no concept of the future, of old age, of mellow times and retirement with family, children and friends. Capone may have appeared to the world as a leader, but internally, he was a reckless, rudderless ship.

The Capone mob now numbered over 1000 members, the majority of them stone-cold killers. Al was a murderer, a pimp, an extortionist and a bootlegger. He built a fearsome reputation in the ruthless gang rivalries of the period, struggling to acquire and retain "racketeering rights" to several areas of Chicago. That reputation grew as rival gangs were eliminated or nullified.

His mentors gone, Capone surrounded himself with his most trusted mobsters: Frank Nitti, Machine Gun McGurn and Tony "Big Tuna" Accardo. Paranoia ruled the landscape. Trust became everything. Al felt that if you couldn't trust your bodyguards, you would end up whacked. His trust was well placed with his inner circle, and that trust was returned equally.

But even so, Al had to be careful. There were many attempts to rub him out. On one occasion, the Bugs Moran gang sent a whole motorcade of machine-gun-happy mobsters past his Cicero headquarters. Over 1000 rounds were fired into the building, but Al escaped without a scratch.

As a show of machismo, Al rarely carried firearms, but was never without at least two bodyguards, usually more. As viciously as he dealt with his enemies, his treatment of disloyal employees was even worse. His most famous personal retribution involved the killing of three of his own men: John Scalise, Albert Anselmi and "Hop Toad" Giunta. These three men were conspiring to have Capone eliminated, but Al got wise to their scheme. Capone invited them to a banquet and, after the meal, pulled out a club and personally bashed in their brains on the dinner table. Police who discovered their bodies later on said that they had never seen men so disfigured by human brutality.

Another example of Al taking matters into his own hands concerned the murder of Billy McSwiggin, a young prosecutor who attempted to pin the Joe Howard murder on Capone. McSwiggin and three other young, Irish civilians hypocritically went out on a drinking binge one night, and unknowingly ended up in Cicero, in one of Capone's own speakeasies. Al was beside himself with rage and indignity, thinking that this was an act of defiant disrespect on McSwiggin's part.

As McSwiggin and his party departed, they were met by Capone and his henchmen, and a hale of tommy gun bullets. Killing a prosecutor was gutsy stuff, crazy stuff, but once it was done, it was done. Public outcry against mob violence rose to a fever pitch, and everyone in the country knew that Capone was somehow involved.

Despite this, not a shred of evidence could be found to indict Capone and once again, the original "Teflon Don" skated free. Nonetheless, another attempt at a police-versus-Capone war was started by Chicago's finest as they raided many of Al's bordellos and speakeasies, oftentimes setting fire to the buildings in retaliation.

Al went into hiding for three months, fearing the raw numbers that were stacked against him in a war that he felt he could not win. It was reported that 300 detectives were on the lookout for him all over the country, even crossing the ocean to Italy, yet nowhere could he be found.

Ironically, Al did not stray far, lamming it up in Chicago Heights and later, Lansing, Michigan. When the heat died down a bit, he reemerged and turned himself in, knowing full well that there was insufficient evidence to indict him. A free man once more, it was business as usual again for the King of Chicago.

Hymie Weiss was Bugs Moran's right-hand man, and he had been one of the shooters in both the botched attempt on Johnny Torrio's life and the futile, military-style attack on Al in Cicero. Despite his name, which, like that of most mobsters, was invented, Hymie was not Jewish, but rather a Polish Catholic. When Capone came back to face the music in the McSwiggin murder, he soon thereafter sought out Weiss in an apparent attempt to forge a peace. They met and all went as planned, the two parting amicably, if warily. The next day, Capone's men cut Weiss down with machine gun fire.

But all of this pales in comparison to the most famous of

Al Capone's murderous acts, the St. Valentine's Day Massacre. Until the day he died, Capone could never quite figure out how or why this particular assassination became such a part of American mobster folklore. For one thing, he had fairly little to do with it, and was most certainly not there. The massacre was, in fact, the brainchild of Machine Gun McGurn, who, with Frank Nitti, was running things in Chicago while Al set up his family in their newly purchased vacation home in Florida. Bugs Moran had consistently bedeviled the Capone gang, and McGurn, for one, had just about had it.

McGurn, with the blessing of Capone, put together a crack team of assassins. The plan was for an unaffiliated bootlegger to invite Moran and his gang to a garage, to buy some very good whiskey at a bargain basement price. The meeting date was set for Valentine's Day, February 14, 1929. The hit men wore police uniforms, giving the impression of a raid, and granting Capone's men the element of surprise. As this was expected to be a very major killing, even McGurn arranged to be far from the scene when it happened, checking into a hotel with his girlfriend around the time it was to occur.

Two of the hitters were out-of-towners from Detroit. While this assisted in the police illusion, it caused the accuracy and efficiency of the plot to falter. The two Motor City men thought they saw Moran enter the garage, and signaled that the assassination was a "go." All went according to plan. The faux policemen entered and the seven men of Moran's gang dutifully lined up against a wall in typical "hands against the wall and spread 'em while we search you" fashion.

Then, the fireworks began. Perhaps it was the execution-style mass murder of so many men at one time, none of them able to defend themselves. Maybe it was the raw number of bullets lodged into the victims. But this became the hit that turned a country, which had come to hate Prohibition and laud bootleggers like Capone, into one that despised Public Enemy Number One. No amount of public relations could rehabilitate his image after this day, despite his ironclad alibi of being in Miami at the time the hit occurred.

Two of the four hit men slipped on trench coats, put their hands in the air, and walked ahead of the two still in uniform. Seeing this, despite the gunfire, people outside the garage thought it was a successful raid on bootleggers, and thought nothing much of it as the four drove away in a stolen police car.

Moran benefited from tardiness, arriving just as Capone's "police" entered the building. Sensing not a gunfight but a standard Prohibition raid, he hightailed it out of sight before the action began, much to his good fortune. With Capone in Florida and McGurn in a hotel, no charges were ever brought against anyone in the St. Valentine's Day Massacre.

I doubt that even Al Capone himself knew the total number of men he personally killed, and there's even less of a chance that any number could be attached to how many murders he ordered, or how many were simply done on his behalf. Most crime historians claim that nearly all, if not all, were done by fellow "soldiers"—mobsters themselves as opposed to normal, law-abiding citizens. Nonetheless, the number is high.

Furthermore, I would find it impossible to come to terms with, were I to know that a member of my immediate family had killed even one solitary person. The totality of numbers numbs one to the act itself—the taking of a life, the single vilest

237

act a human can commit. All societies have been based primarily upon this single code of conduct, above all others.

Here I stand, amidst a pool of blood, thinking upon the lives of faceless men, who were born and died long before I was even conceived. As I wonder whether I am the grandchild of Alphonse Capone, I must also imagine the existence of the grandchildren of Frankie Yale, Big Jim Colosimo, Dion O'Banion, Joe Howard, Pegleg Lonergan, John Scalise, Albert Anselmi, Hop Toad Giunta and Billy McSwiggin. All these grandfathers, murdered by the hand of a man I imagine to be my own grandfather. It chills me.

If Capone's blood runs through me, it is blood tainted by the bloodshed of others, whether Al Capone felt they deserved it or not. This I have to live with. This, for me, is not a choice, not a reach for a degree of fame or notoriety. It is more of a burden, a cross of shame. If I am able finally to find it to be unassailably true someday, and even if I'm not, I know I have the responsibility to live a life of peace and human fellowship, to cause no harm to others.

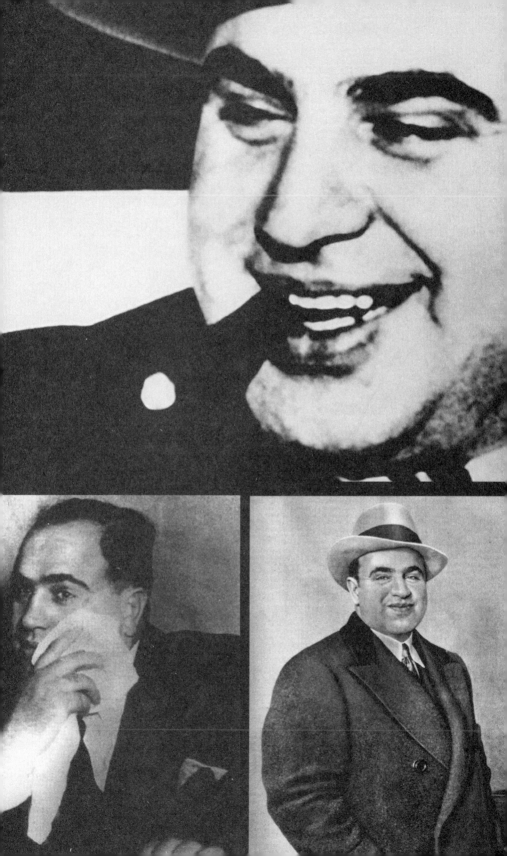

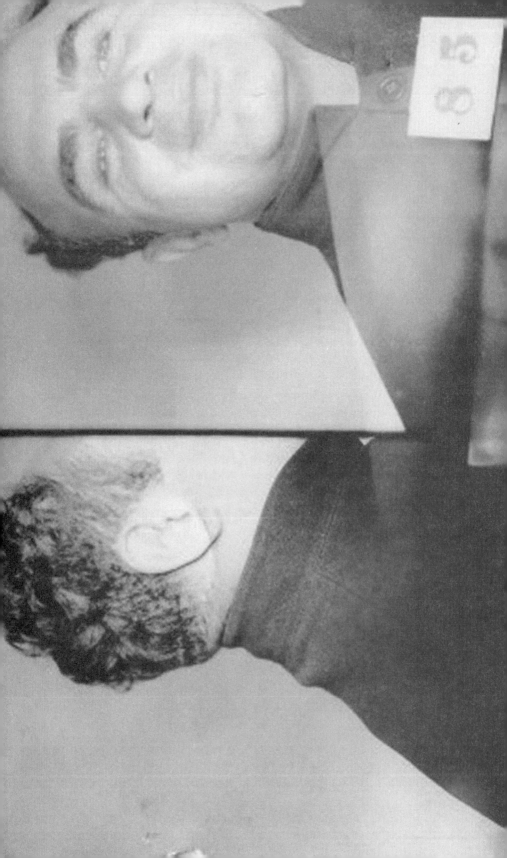

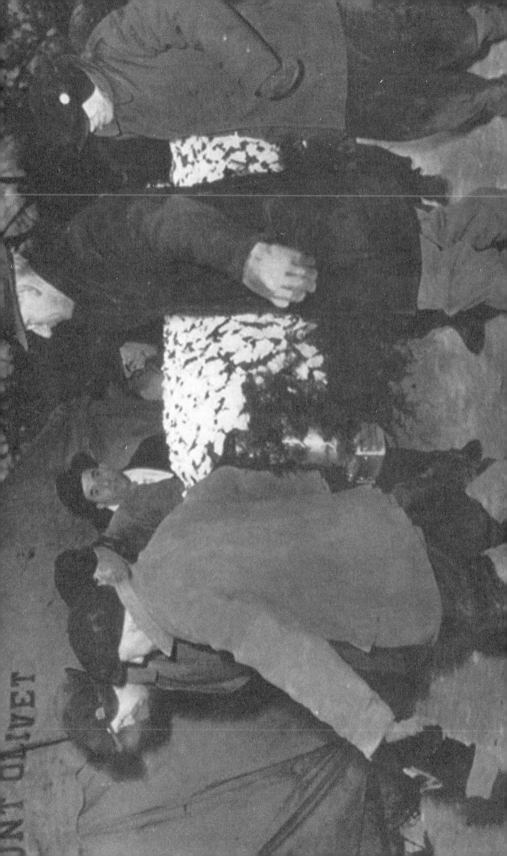

Al Capone

XVIII

BIG AL?

I do not deny that this chapter is somewhat a flight of fancy. Over the years, I've heard many gay men say, "Everyone's gay. There are just those who know it and those who haven't figured it out yet," or words to that effect. It's an extreme viewpoint, and one I don't tend to agree with, but the aspect of it that pervades the gay community is to wonder and imagine who is and who isn't gay, leaning far more on the side of, "Oh yeah, he *definitely* is." Hell, privately, we out everybody. It's a parlor game.

La Costa Nostra is, at its heart, Italian, macho and Catholic. None of this abides well with homosexuality. There are certainly no "out" gay Mafioso, or at least none that I am aware of. Still, despite what critics say about the death of good investigative reporting, the outing or near-outing of gay mobsters is more a part of today's more lurid press than what was being reported in Capone's day.

As stated innumerable times, Al claimed to have only one legitimate child, Sonny. My father believed he was another son—legitimate or otherwise—and there have been rumors of others, as well as rumors of back alley abortions forced upon various mistresses and prostitutes by Big Al.

Yet, Al only having one child with Mae, his wife, still stands out starkly from his mob contemporaries of the '20s and '30s. These Italians, as well as their Irish counterparts, regularly produced huge broods of offspring. I am eliminating the possibility of sterility, because if Al and Mae could have one child, they could have had more.

So why only one child? Well, let's also take into consideration the particulars of Al's criminal lifestyle. While some mobsters were family men (no play on words), Al basically lived apart from Mae. He lived primarily in the Lexington and the Metropole Hotels in Chicago, as well as, of course, staying in hotels when he traveled. Mae lived in the Capone homestead on Prairie Avenue in Chicago, alone. When Al traveled, Mae stayed behind.

Now, to give him the benefit of the doubt, Al most certainly wanted to shield his wife—and his mother, for that matter, who lived with Mae on Prairie Avenue as well, along with Sonny—from the assassination attempts on his life that were so very frequent. But, for as logical as this was, Al's enemies certainly had to have known that Mae, his mother and Sonny were targets that were just as desirable as Al. One of the most chilling and clichéd intimidation tactics for de-clawing an enemy is to threaten his family. It goes without saying that Al must have had Prairie Avenue surrounded by bodyguards as much as he was guarded himself.

Al's attentions to the details of personal protection are legend. The reinforced walls, ceilings and floors of the Lexington and Metropole hotel rooms. The bodyguards above, below and on every side of him. Logic begs the question: would it not have been more cost-efficient to keep close to his family, and only have to pay one set of bodyguards, instead of two?

Mae and Sonny were trotted out for show, for public relations only. Outside of that, they lived a life apart from Al, despite living in the very same city. This was *not* typical of a Mafia chieftain.

And so I let my "gay-dar" wander. Al lived apart from his wife. Mae was a beautiful woman, the perfect "beard—a woman who accompanies a gay man in order for him to look like a straight playboy. Al had a high-pitched speaking voice, as do I. He is often described as being soft-spoken and genteel in his ways and mannerisms, a stark contrast to the violence he rained down upon the world. Do we describe these as "effeminate" traits?

Al's bodyguards—they have been described as huge, muscular, yet fashionably well dressed and coifed. Al set up gyms for them to keep in tip-top shape, yet Al himself never seemed to indulge much in bodybuilding. Why would a straight man want always to surround himself with hunky, young musclemen?

While most gay sex scandals within the Mafia are more germane to our modern era, we must recall the saga of the man who should have been Capone's and the Mafia's main nemesis during the '20s, '30s and up until his death in the early 1970s: J. Edgar Hoover. In the 1950s, FBI Director Hoover stunned law enforcement nationwide with his public pronouncement that "there is no such thing as organized crime in the United States."

It is now accepted as fact that Hoover was a homosexual, who was blackmailed by the Mafia through the possession of secretly taken photographs of him and his lover Clyde Tolson, the second-in-command at the FBI. Hoover and Tolson lived together as husband and wife for nearly 40 years and Tolson, who survived Hoover, was the sole beneficiary of his estate. They are buried together in our nation's oldest national cemetery, the Congressional Cemetery in Washington, D. C.

Could there have been a gay *quid pro quo* between Capone and Hoover? The phrase "Gay Mafia" is used improperly and derisively today to describe gay—or allegedly gay—power brokers in Hollywood, assumed to work together, as all ethnic, racial, religious and now sexually-oriented groups are accused of "helping each other out" clannishly. Indeed, the Mafia itself has cast a dark shadow upon all Italian-Americans, most of whom are assumed to be "mobbed up," particularly if they become financially successful.

Hoover is also tarred with the allegation of being a transvestite, making him, posthumously, the butt of many comedians' jokes, particularly considering his zaftig frame and unappealing looks. Ironically, a mobbed up member of today's FBI Ten Most Wanted List is said to be lamming it by prancing around the world in drag, living in various gay neighborhoods.

"Whitey" Bulger, Boston's most famous mobster—and brother of the former State Senate President and politically appointed President of the University of Massachusetts, Billy Bulger—has been on the run since 1995. Boston writer and radio personality Howie Carr writes that Bulger began his life

of crime as a gay hustler, eventually "rolling johns"—beating up
those who paid for his sexual services—while living in Bay
Village, a famous gay neighborhood in Boston.

Bulger, like any mobster, felt the need to keep his sexuality
closeted and indeed, there are those today who will contest his
leanings. Bulger lived out of wedlock with the same woman for
30 years. She had children that Whitey raised as his own, but
he has no blood heirs. Again, a perfect beard.

Whitey has been charged with RICO (federal racketeering) violations, extortion, money laundering, distribution of
narcotics and 18 counts of murder. For decades, he was the
recognized kingpin of all Boston organized crime, protected
from prosecution by his politically connected brother and a
relationship with the FBI whereby he snitched to a closeted
gay FBI agent, whom he would meet in area gay bars, about his
criminal rivals.

Today, FBI reports prompt agents worldwide to be on the
lookout for Whitey Bulger in known gay neighbors, his favorite
hangout. Edward J. Mackenzie, author of *Street Soldier: My
Life as an Enforcer for Whitey Bulger and the Irish Mob*,
describes Bulger as a transvestite. Thus, a man who today is on
the same FBI short list as Osama Bin Laden is most likely
living in a gay neighborhood, dressed like a woman.

J. Edgar Hoover would be proud.

Greg Scarpa, a hitman for the Colombo Mafia Family,
died of AIDS in 1994. It is now known that J. Edgar Hoover
recruited Scarpa as an informant in 1961. In 1964, Hoover
sent Scarpa to Mississippi, where he placed the barrel of an FBI
agent's revolver into the mouth of a member of the Ku Klux

Klan, threatening to blow the man's brains out if he did not reveal the location of the bodies of three missing civil rights activists. For solving this crime, Scarpa was rewarded by literally being given a license to commit any crime with impunity, much as had Whitey Bulger, which Scarpa did for decades from his Bensonhurst headquarters which he named—you can't make this stuff up—the "Wimpy Boys Social Club."

In the mid-1990s, *Spy* magazine devoted a story to the subject of homosexuals within the Mafia, and named several examples from recent years. Also during that time, associates of convicted Gambino family Godfather John Gotti investigated reports that former underboss Sammy "The Bull" Gravano was gay, and had committed more than the 19 murders he confessed to when he agreed to testify against Gotti.

Gravano's sexual appetite was said to have been fueled by his abuse of anabolic steroids, powerful muscle-building drugs that induce side effects of violent behavior, as well as an increase in sexual libido. When Gravano was arrested for his role in selling drugs to kids in Arizona, anabolic steroids were among the illegal items found in his possession. It is no wonder that Sammy the Bull has a higher price on his head than any other mob informant.

In 2000, *Village Voice* reporter Wayne Barrett created a sensation when he published a biography of New York City Mayor Rudy Giuliani, which included details that relatives of the mayor were members of the Mafia. Among those named was Giuliani's cousin, Lewis D'Avanzo, a gay mobster who was shot dead in a confrontation with the FBI.

The DeCavalcante crime family of New Jersey has

provided the inspiration for the HBO hit series *The Sopranos*. During the course of investigations, agents of the FBI tape-recorded members of the "family" talking about the hit television series and how they believed their own activities were represented in the program.

Anthony Capo, a member of the DeCavalcante mob, admitted in court that in 1992, he and other members of the gang murdered the acting boss of the family, "Johnny Boy" D'Amato, because of his gay activities. D'Amato allegedly had a wife and a girlfriend, and it was the girlfriend who complained to Capo and others that Johnny Boy was frequenting sex clubs, where he would sometimes have sex with other men. The sex clubs in question operate throughout the New York and New Jersey area, and some are run by the mob.

Capo told the jury that there was concern among members of the family that if the other Mafia crews in the region found out about D'Amato's gay behavior, it would cause them to lose respect for the DeCavalcantes. Killing a mob boss without permission from the "commission" representing New York's five Mafia families is, however, against Mafia protocol, so Capo claimed the members of the murder conspiracy agreed to accomplish it quietly, without permission and without acknowledging responsibility.

Capo alleged that *consigliere* (family advisor) Stefano Vitabile approved of the hit. The murder was carried out, according to Capo, when he and an associate picked up D'Amato at his girlfriend's house in Brooklyn. The New Jersey mob boss then climbed into the back of the car, and Capo turned from the front and shot him several times with his gun. It is not just a figment of television writers, then, that the Mafia kills their own if they happen to be gay. *The Sopranos* literally copied this very story line in a series of episodes in 2006.

It is difficult to discuss gay culture without mentioning gay nightclubs and bars. Pre-Stonewall (a New York City gay club, and site of famous gay rights riots in the 1960's), gay clubs were incredibly hush-hush, *à la* speakeasies, and continued to require that same sort of, "Knock knock," "Who is it?" "Vinny sent me," special club membership in order to avoid overzealous police vice squads and assorted Bible thumpers.

This being said, many gay clubs had been and continue to be owned by the Mafia. I do not know how far back this goes, but I do know this: one of the oldest gay establishments in Chicago was owned by...Al Capone, and managed by his brother, Ralph.

The Shoreline 7, at 7 W. Division was really called the Shoreline, but on the matchbooks, it said "Shoreline," then underneath, the number seven, then "West Division," so everyone called it the Shoreline 7. It was regarded as a neat, fun place featuring drag shows—men dressed as women (again, Mr. Hoover). Ralph Capone ran it into the 1960s, not bothering to invest much into it, and so by the end of its days, it became quite the run-down, seedy place. Did Alphonse give his blessing upon this particular type of enterprise? Was he, perhaps, even the first Mafioso to engage in such industry? If so, it would make him an icon in gay American history.

Speaking briefly of Stonewall, it is ironic that there was a Mafia/J. Edgar Hoover connection there as well. The Stonewall Inn was also Mafia-owned, by a connected gentleman by the name of Tony Lauria. Despite its being a dump with watered-down, overpriced drinks, the New York gay crowd packed into the Stonewall because of the relief of knowing that with the Laurias paying off the cops, the place was unlikely to be raided, which would cause embarrassment to the closeted queens, many of them married and living a lie in the suburbs.

The primary protector of the Stonewall, though, was a mobster by the name of Ed "The Skull" Murphy, who is credited with having the photographic goods on J. Edgar Hoover. This became Murphy's specialty. Other habitual denizens of the Stonewall were closeted Wall Street types. Murphy threatened them as well, vowing to protect their anonymity, but extracting, in return, things of far greater value than a place to have a drink and cruise.

Murphy had these Wall Street tycoons stealing negotiable bearer bonds for him, which he smuggled out of the country and cashed. Suddenly, Interpol was involved in the investigation. Even J. Edgar Hoover could not control Interpol and indeed, the scandal would have reached legendary proportions if he were to be implicated, or if Interpol put the squeeze on Murphy.

The Stonewall raids occurred, gay men of New York rioted in retaliation, and the modern gay liberation movement began. The raids turned up no Ed "The Skull" and no strong leads on the bond stealing case. I can only imagine, though, how juicy it would have been if they had.

It is no longer assumed that homosexuality is a mental disorder or something that one "gets." The accepted notion is that the sexuality of gay men is set from birth. Indeed, as scientists are discovering the "fat gene" and the "cancer gene," they are also zeroing in on the "gay gene." That being said, I am a gay man. Perhaps Al Capone was as well. Or perhaps he was bi,

257

although there is a saying, "Bi today, gay tomorrow."

I also continue to question my father's sexuality. He remains a mystery wrapped in an enigma on so many fronts, his sexual relationships included. There is a joke where, when confronted by discussion of a "gay gene," someone responds, "But how can that be? Gays don't multiply." But yes, some do.

And so I know who I am. What I wonder is, am I also, in this respect, a genetic link to my father? A genetic link to my grandfather, Al Capone? To one, the other, both, or neither? I wonder.

Sister, dad and me

XIX

THE CHAPTER THAT NEVER ENDS

My father, William "Billy" Knight, Jr., had never been a particularly healthy man. He was also quite a bit older than my mother. Even as a child, somewhere deep in the recesses of my mind, I must have imagined she would out-live him, horrible as that thought may have seemed.

Yes, he led the truck driver's lonely existence, leaving us for weeks at a time but, without trying to overuse a cliché, the time he spent with my sister and me was quality time. He had his passions, and he shared them with me. He loved boats and boating. He was probably more into the Boy Scouts as an adult volunteer than I was as an actual Scout. Despite his arthritis, he happily slept on the hard ground on every camping trip we scheduled. Before recycling became mandatory, he would lead his own personal recycling drives, picking up metal, cashing it in, and contributing the proceeds to the Boy Scouts of America and our local troop.

During my journey into the land of Capone, I discovered that Sonny Capone was driven out of the Boy Scouts, shunned because of his father's infamy. Reading that, it brought back what for me were fond childhood memories. How ironic.

My last memories of my father involved my sister and me waiting, as always, for him to return from one of those infamous truck driving trips. We swung on our swing set on a warm summer's day, excited with the anticipation that his arrival always conjured up within us. There had been talk in our house of a typical New Jersey summer vacation—a few days down at Seaside Heights, on the inimitable Jersey shore.

I vaguely recall his arrival being delayed, although with my father, there was not usually such a thing as a definite schedule. His comings and goings were always somewhat of a mystery. We'd be led to believe he'd be home on Thursday; he'd come home on Saturday. It had ceased to be an issue of concern. Thus, vacation plans were usually left until the last minute.

When he came home, we packed up the car and drove down the shore. My father always chugged down aspirin and other over-the-counter pain relievers like candy, but after a stop at a roadside burger joint, he complained of stomach pains. He switched from aspirin to Tums and the trek continued.

We reached our destination, my sister and I excited as any two kids could be, checking into a motel at the ocean's edge, complete with its own swimming pool if we preferred to switch from salt water to fresh. No sooner did we open the door to our room than our father began having a heart attack. He went to the bed and laid down. Confused and as ineffectual as any 13-year-old, I simply went to him and held his hand while my mother and sister ran to get help.

He couldn't really tell me what to do, so I reached into his pocket and pulled out that trusty bottle of aspirin and poured a bunch into his hand. He looked me in the eye and gasped a prayer. I told him that I loved him as he slipped into unconsciousness.

The door ajar, a woman in a nearby room came upon us and began administering CPR. Soon, the ambulance came, and the paramedics placed him on a stretcher, shooing me out of the room as they worked on my father. My mother, my sister and I went down to the sidewalk in front of the motel and stood by the ambulance, huddled together, knowing that no matter what, this was where the paramedics would eventually be returning.

Finally, they rolled the gurney out of the room and brought him toward us. None of us had any idea whether he was alive or dead, conscious or unconscious, but we were relieved to find, as he got closer, that he was indeed awake and somewhat alert. He was unable to say a word, but as they put him in the back of the ambulance, he turned his head and gave the three of us one last glance. It was not something I imagined; he stared right at us, his eyes meeting ours. He then straightened his head as the paramedics carefully closed the doors and began to pull out. I would later discover that he died, unable to be revived once more, in the back of that ambulance, on the way to the hospital where my mother drove to meet him.

In all the tumult, my sister and I stayed behind, watched over by the kindly motel manager at this little, mom-and-pop family resort by the sea. Our mother would later return to tell us how upset she was at our father's passing, and how she had screamed and yelled at the doctors, as if there were more that they could have done, despite the fact that he was dead before he even reached their care.

A priest came by our hotel room to say prayers with us—a surreal scene to be sure. My mother was even more unglued than usual, but any other reaction from her would have been even less appropriate. She was far too distraught to turn around and drive us immediately back home, so she called her brother, who arranged to come down the following day to pick us all up. Appropriately enough, it rained like the dickens the next day as we drove home. The sunshine and excitement of the day before was long gone.

Once we got home, my mother went about the unpleasant business of coordinating a funeral. The next time I saw my father, he lay in a coffin, an American flag draped over him in appreciation of his military service during World War II. My reaction was typical—I had lost my father, my heart ached, and I knew I would never be the same.

I've been to many wakes and funerals since, but my father was waked for three days and nights—something I've never seen before or since. During each scheduled visitation, the large, mansion-like funeral parlor was filled to the brim with respectful mourners. Nearly every face I had seen during my young life, I saw again, paying their respects to a man who, I had conjectured, had earned their love and respect.

Were there faces that were unfamiliar to me? Absolutely. As banal as that was to me then, it entices and intrigues me today. Were my mother, my sister and I the only blood relatives of my father who had been there those three days and nights? Or were there old faces from his past, people who stealthily snuck in, said a regretful prayer, and then left back into the darkness of anonymity? I may never know.

Some faces made their presences known. A bigwig from Union Carbide, the company my father drove for, came in, so very well dressed, and presented a check to my mother in gratitude for my father's years of faithful service. I overheard people introducing themselves as being from out of town— far, far out of town—people I could only assume at the time were businesspeople he dealt with at the other end of his trucking runs.

Our next-door neighbor, a male gym teacher who considered himself the local stud, came by and unabashedly began hitting on my mother, right there in the funeral home. Whatever bad things I have said about my mother, she was a very attractive woman and I suppose this gym teacher was afraid that if he didn't step up in line and make his interest known quickly, someone else might sweep in before him. Nonetheless, it was obviously inappropriate, and some of my father's true friends began discussing it among themselves: "I've got a baseball bat in the back of my trunk. Think I should go get it and take Mr. Muscles out back, and let him have it?"

I often wonder whether, in the weeks before his passing, my father knew his time on this earth would soon be up. Again, his poor health made his biological age far older than his chronological age. My secret dream has been that he was anticipating just the right moment to sit down with me, his 13-year-old son, to tell me the truth of his lineage, of who he really was, and what that all meant to me. In my dreams, that scene was to have occurred if only he had lived a few days longer. Thirteen is a biblical age of maturity, a time when a boy is said to become a man. The time was right. But the moment never came.

Shortly before we'd left on vacation, my father had finally traded in the ratty, old pickup truck he'd driven, for a shiny new one. Such things are very exciting in a young boy's life, and Dad was so proud of that new, big purchase. He'd brought me over to the dealership to see it—a beautiful Dodge Ram with an AM-FM radio (a real luxury for him), airconditioning (ditto), and an automatic transmission.

The automatic transmission had been for me. At the tender age of 13, my father was already teaching me to drive, letting me tool around where he parked his rig. This new pick-up with an automatic would be so much easier for me.

We had driven the pick-up back to where he'd parked his rig, and stashed it away out of sight. He'd also had a station wagon, which was the primary family car. One of my last memories of me and my father, just the two of us alone, is of us looking back at that new pick-up, admiring it. For all the upgrades and options he'd put into it, one thing was oddly amiss: it was without a bumper. Why was that? I have no idea. Perhaps he'd gotten a deal on it; I don't know.

So, we'd stared at this almost-perfect, new vehicle, and he'd said to me, "We really need to get that thing a new bumper. A nice, new, shiny, chrome bumper. What do you think?" Of course, I'd agreed excitedly. On the eve of his last trip, he'd still been making plans.

This stands in contrast to something we found out shortly after his funeral. It seems that the reason my father was late coming home from his last run was that he'd had some sort of heart episode while on the road, and had spent his last three days sick in bed in a motel somewhere, clinging to life. He'd refused medical care and would not allow himself to be admitted to the hospital, illogical as that may seem.

The theory of his friends, and those he confided in, was that he'd just wanted to get well enough to come back to New Jersey, so that he could die at home, with his loved ones around him. Why he'd let on that nothing was wrong, and that it was fine for us all to go on vacation, remains a mystery to me, but it seems that he'd wanted his last visual images of us to be smiling and happy, just as that new truck that I was going to drive while underage made me so very happy as well.

It's a romantic concept, but with only one missing piece: why didn't he make time to tell me more about himself? I would have traded in all the vacations and new trucks in the world for that sort of closure.

I reflect back today on my father with a mixture of feelings—all of them intense, many of them conflicted. There is only one thing that remains constant: I miss him. While alive, he was only slightly more of a mystery to me than most fathers are to their sons. The name "Capone" was never said in my presence, and were I not to have been the one to bring it up in later years, around my mother, it would never be spoken in her presence or in her home.

For years, my main focus regarding the loss of my father was in regard to the torture my mother had put my sister and me through. Indeed, the worst of it had happened, ironically, while he was still alive. But, I believe my sister and I were working toward mustering up the courage to tell my father more and more about it, and, perhaps, he would have done more to save us from it. At the very least, he and I could have talked about it man to man, rather than man to child.

Check a dictionary and you will find that the word "dignity" means being worthy of esteem or honor—being highly valued. If this were to be taken literally, it would imply that an infant has less dignity than an adult, and is destined to achieve virtually nothing until far older.

However, any newborn already has his or her dignity, as he or she has a soul, and the dignity of a human soul is the birthright of all human beings. Dignity is not a quality of being highly valued, but it is the highest human value itself. Unfortunately, most people tend to acquire their dignity from the judgments of other people. For years, I devalued my own self because I allowed my mother's words to stick within my ears, making me feel like less of a person, less of a human being.

I do not know for sure how my father's true heritage plays into my mother's treatment of my sister and me. Since beginning this journey, I have confronted her with my discoveries, and she has admitted it: my father was Al Capone's son. She's not particularly proud of it; she seems to have not confided in anyone else about it. Most children might be tempted to leave things alone at that, and were I to be told almost anything else about my father's roots, I might be persuaded to do just that. But, two issues remain: one, the notoriety, and two, my insatiable thirst for the truth.

Regarding the notoriety, it has absolutely nothing to do with bragging rights or petitions for hidden money (hello, Geraldo! Want to open some more vaults with me?). It's just that I am a social man, a person who enjoys the company of others. For all the psychoses my mother flung upon me, I am not a hermit. Perhaps I find in friends the love and affection I should have been getting from her.

CHRIS W KNIGHT

So then, what would happen to your relationship with a friend were he to tell you he was the secret son of, say, Charles Manson? Two reactions stand out: fear or disbelief. Neither is good. Granted, I have already confided these tales in good, true friends, and they have remained supportive, as all good friends should. But what about the new person I meet next week, or the week after? At what point can I open up? At what point do I stick my finger in the proverbial fan and risk getting it cut off when he thinks I'm some kind of loony or another?

Life is supposed to be a search for truth. What happens when absolute, proven truth appears almost impossible to attain?

Like most things in my life, this withholding of the whole truth continues to divide my mother and me. It is just one more thing that she can hang over me, tantalize me with and deny me. Whenever I bring it up, she says something on the order of, "Yes, that was your grandfather. So what? I don't want to talk about it." Since my search began, my mother and I have spoken less and less, because this is all I really want to talk to her about. This is what plagues my dreams.

Which brings me back to dignity. Physical and mental torture is a primal, unquestionable method by which someone destroys the dignity of another. So, too, with withholding important truths from that person. Consider the mental torture that prisoners of war face. One of the first ways in which the spirit is broken is to tell the prisoner, "No one is coming to get you. There will be no rescue. Your comrades have left you behind to die. They no longer care about you. Your situation is hopeless."

This, in effect, was my childhood. Now, as an adult, as I seek the whole truth of my existence, my mother again holds

SON OF SCARFACE

over my head that same sort of perverse power. "I will not answer your questions. I will not tell you any more." Further destruction of dignity.

And yes, there is the issue of money. Not Capone money that I would ever seek from anyone outside the four walls of my childhood home, but the money I know my mother to possess. The gold bullion from the secret safe deposit box I saw for an instant, before she shooed me away. How much was in there? Where is it now? My sister and I are her only heirs, but what will we find when she's gone? Will it have been promised to some young gigolo she may meet between now and her demise? Or will it be the revenge of the truly hateful and miserly, hidden or buried beneath mattresses or in ditches, who knows where?

Shortly after my father's death, my mother went on a ravenous search for an old will—emphasis on "old." I was only 13 at the time, but it seemed to me even then that she was bullying and screaming at lawyers, attempting to find not necessarily my father's latest will, but some other will that contoured his wishes to hers. Maybe it was a will drawn up before my sister or I were even born. I don't know. At this point in my life, neither of us has ever received any lump sum upon reaching the age of 18, 21 or 25—the typical bench-marks of chronological maturity. Nor did my sister receive anything of the sort when she married or gave birth, another common inheritance strategy (rather unfair to a gay man such as myself).

So, where's the money? *Is* there any money? And in searching for it and attempting to account for it, where exactly did my father's money come from in the first place?

Recently, while perusing the TV listings, I read about an

upcoming Oprah Winfrey special. In it, she talked about genealogy, tracing one's roots, and finding out one's individual truth. She hypothesized that obtaining information on your family's past could help enhance your dignity. She discussed how her ancestors paved the path for her being here and lit the way to her destiny.

This hit home with me, as I was trying to find the truth about *my* ancestors. It has been important for me to find the truth about my father because he tried to give my sister and me dignity.

And then, on another point, how come Oprah can trace *her* family's heritage all the way back to Africa, to when they were abducted to be sold as slaves in America, and I can't find information on my father, William G. Knight, Jr., allegedly born in the United States of America in the 20th century? Not a single damn thing. Oprah has pictures, that were found by her genealogists, of her great-great-great-great-grandparents. Me...nothing.

Of course, we all know that the answer is money, and Oprah has more than the GNP of some small nations. But then again, I have also spent money on genealogists, private detectives and what have you. Hello, Al Capone; you did a damn good job of covering your tracks!

When I began this expedition, it was a simultaneous project. I began the search, and I began this diary of that search. My expectation was that I would chronicle the journey for truth as it played out in real time. It was an exciting notion. I figured that at the end of the road, I would end up either with a *eureka!* moment of unquestionable affirmation, or something akin to Geraldo's infamous empty vault.

271

I have ended up with neither. What I have is circumstantial evidence. In legal parlance, I probably have enough to win a civil trial, but not a criminal one. I remain without proof beyond a reasonable doubt. I only have simple proof, sufficient to make most people say, "Yeah, it looks like it's probably true. There are far too many links, bits, pieces and question marks all leading to the same conclusion for that conclusion to not have any validity."

It is the truth that my father's only living wife knows to be true; so, too, his best friend John, his close friend, my Uncle on my mother's side and the late Thor, perhaps his best friend from decades ago. Even friends from his teens who are still alive all echo the same conclusion: Billy Knight was the son of Al Capone, Boss of Bosses, King of Chicago, and Public Enemy Number One.

But I cannot prove it. I can also not disprove it. I know that DNA is the ultimate answer, but living people, accepted as known Capone heirs, were discovered by me or those in my network, only to disappear soon after. None of them want anything to do with this quest. It's nothing personal; I know that. All of them have one thing in common. None of them trumpets their own linage to the man behind the St. Valentine's Day Massacre. Each of them shies away at the first mention of their own blood ties to Scarface, even before I mention the reason behind my seeking them out. None has been willing to do a DNA test to see if they are a match with me.

Some nights, I get so desperate, I finger the phone, toying with the idea of hiring a private detective to hunt them down and force from them a piece of DNA—a hair from the shoulder of their coat or whatever. This is the craziness that goes through the mind of a normally sane person who is simply wishing to put to rest the most basic aspect of his being—who am I, and how did I get here?

My own DNA has been logged in and analyzed. Italian blood runs through me. Not 100 percent, of course, but enough to venture that one of my grandparents could be Italian. I have toyed with delaying the release of this book with the final entry, the definitive knowledge and proof that I am, unquestionably, the grandson of Alphonse Capone. But now, I know that the acquisition of such proof, beyond any reasonable doubt, may take years, many more years. So, what do I do in the meantime?

No, my goal has never been to put out a book, to become an author. This is simply my chronicle, one I needed to keep in order to collect my thoughts and preserve my feelings. That being said, I know what I feel now versus how I felt when this all began.

I am Al Capone's grandchild.

When I look in my mirror, my own face stares back at me. But, shadow images also creep into the picture. I see my father, smiling, proud of me for never giving up, for being forthright and vigilant. I also see *his* father, Al Capone. His face is a cliché, a mixture of familiar images from famed photographs and newspapers. His expression betrays no specific feeling toward me or my father. It is simply that face, that famous/infamous face, with the scar on the cheek. I see myself, and I see all of these images.

The *real* Capone legacy has become lost with time—a historically short time, when one considers it. I can only compare it to that of Adolph Hitler. "Hitler" was a fairly common

Germanic name prior to World War II. During and after the war, most Americans with that name changed it, to avoid persecution by association with it. While every person in the world has heard of Adolph Hitler, his distant relatives are now scattered and hidden, living under aliases and changed names. His family legacy no longer exists, a curse that he brought upon his house by his murderous tyranny.

Today, most every city in America has a pizza place or Italian restaurant named "Capone's." The owners are rarely named Capone, but rather use some cartoonish image of Alphonse to promote their eatery. It is one thing to laugh at a picture of Al Capone, cartoon gangster with a scar on his cheek and a tommy gun in his hand—or a singing, dancing, mincing Adolph Hitler from the Mel Brooks musical *The Producers*—and another to deal with the real thing.

And so, despite my newfound certainty of who I am, my journey continues. Perhaps there will come a time when I may even bring some sort of rebirth to the image of this man, Capone, this icon of American culture, a man who opened soup kitchens for the poor, despite gunning down his rivals. Like most Mafiosos, Capone kept to the vow of "only killing our own," fellow soldiers in the secret army, providing the kinds of goods and services that may have been illegal but would always remain in demand—booze, broads and similar titillations. Still unsavory, yes, but far less distasteful than the acts of the genocidal Hitler.

I'm thankful that this project has brought me even closer to my sister. Not that we were ever estranged, but it seemed that we were both singularly dealing with the trauma of growing up in our mother's house. We had not really leaned on one another as we should have. But, this is not unusual with abuse. Even though we were witness to the torture both of us went through, we could not discuss it; we could not talk about it. We were both ashamed and embarrassed by it, and as each was the other's eyewitness, we kept that embarrassment when we were around one another.

Now, instead, we talk about it. This book, this search into the life of our father, has given us a protective blanket, under which we can initiate discussion about those years. It broke the ice between us; it made us face the realities we both lived and shared, and it has helped us come to terms with it.

To those of you who read this, understand that I leave now at a point near the end of my journey. It has been a mission of self-discovery, of introspection, and of change and reflection. It has been a search for answers, for truth, and for closure. It has been a search to unveil the mysteries of a man who meant so much to me—my father, William Knight. Whoever he was, I love him with all my heart and always will.

I hope that he had within himself the peace that I seek. I hope that he knew truth, and knew answers to the important questions of life. I pray that he knew who he was, and that he was content with it. For I am the son of William Knight. And William Knight was the son of Al Capone.

Picture of us celebrating Dad's B-Day a week
before he passed away.

-July 21, 1984